GoodFood magazine

101 CHEAP EATS

First published 2003
Published by BBC Books, an imprint of Ebury Publishing

20

Ebury Publishing is a division of the Random House Group Ltd.

Copyright © Woodlands Books Ltd 2003
All photographs © *BBC Good Food Magazine* 2003 and *BBC
Vegetarian Good Food Magazine* 2003

All the recipes contained in this book first appeared in
BBC Good Food Magazine and *BBC Vegetarian Good Food Magazine*.

The Random House Group Ltd Reg. No. 954009

Addresses for companies within the Random House Group Ltd can be
found at www.randomhouse.co.uk

A CIP catalogue record for this book is available from the British Library.

The Random House Group Ltd makes every effort to ensure that the
papers used in our books are made from trees that have been legally
sourced from well-managed and credibly certified forests. Our paper
procurement policy can be found at www.randomhouse.co.uk

Edited by Gilly Cubitt
Commissioning Editor: Vivien Bowler
Project Editors: Rebecca Hardie and Sarah Reece
Designers: Kathryn Gammon and Annette Peppis
Design Manager: Sarah Ponder
Production Controller: Christopher Tinker

Set in Helvetica and ITC Officina San
Printed and bound in Italy by LEGO SpA
Colour origination by Radstock Reproductions Ltd, Midsomer Norton

ISBN 978 0 563 48841 5

GoodFood magazine

101 CHEAP EATS
TRIED-AND-TESTED RECIPES

Editor-in-chief
Orlando Murrin

Contents

Introduction   6

Introduction

As every cook knows, it's not how much money you spend on the ingredients that makes a great meal – it's what you do with them. So we've assembled our favourite low-cost recipes from *BBC Good Food Magazine* to prove that eating on a budget can be far from boring.

Forget beans on toast and jacket potatoes with cheese, we've chosen a selection of stylish meals your family and friends will love that don't require special or luxury ingredients. Using storecupboard essentials and foods in season, we can help you conjure up something special every night of the week, like the *Apple Blackberry Ice Cream Sauce* pictured opposite (see page 192 for recipe), without breaking the bank.

Our cookery teams have tried and tested each recipe to make sure they all work perfectly every time, and they've also kept the cost to a minimum without sacrificing flavour or quantities. Each recipe comes with a nutritional breakdown as well, so you can keep an eye on the calorie, fat and salt content.

This book guarantees you'll never be short of quick, low-cost recipes for every season ever again. It takes the stress out of weeknight suppers and you'll be reminded that often the simplest things in life are best.

Orlando Murrin

Editor, *BBC Good Food Magazine*

Conversion tables

NOTES ON THE RECIPES
• Eggs are medium in the UK and Australia (large in America) unless stated otherwise.
• Wash all fresh produce before preparation.

OVEN TEMPERATURES

Gas	°C	Fan °C	°F	Oven temp.
¼	110	90	225	Very cool
½	120	100	250	Very cool
1	140	120	275	Cool or slow
2	150	130	300	Cool or slow
3	160	140	325	Warm
4	180	160	350	Moderate
5	190	170	375	Moderately hot
6	200	180	400	Fairly hot
7	220	200	425	Hot
8	230	210	450	Very hot
9	240	220	475	Very hot

APPROXIMATE WEIGHT CONVERSIONS
• All the recipes in this book list both imperial and metric measurements. Conversions are approximate and have been rounded up or down. Follow one set of measurements only; do not mix the two.
• Cup measurements, which are used by cooks in Australia and America, have not been listed here as they vary from ingredient to ingredient. Please use kitchen scales to measure dry/solid ingredients.

SPOON MEASURES

• Spoon measurements are level unless otherwise specified.

• 1 teaspoon = 5ml

• 1 tablespoon = 15ml

• 1 Australian tablespoon = 20ml (cooks in Australia should measure 3 teaspoons where 1 tablespoon is specified in a recipe)

APPROXIMATE LIQUID CONVERSIONS

metric	imperial	AUS	US
50ml	2fl oz	¼ cup	¼ cup
125ml	4fl oz	½ cup	½ cup
175ml	6fl oz	¾ cup	¾ cup
225ml	8fl oz	1 cup	1 cup
300ml	10fl oz/½ pint	½ pint	1¼ cups
450ml	16fl oz	2 cups	2 cups/1 pint
600ml	20fl oz/1 pint	1 pint	2½ cups
1 litre	35fl oz/1¾ pints	1¾ pints	1 quart

A chunky and satisfying salad,
easily doubled for a crowd.

Tomato Salsa Salad

650g/1lb 7oz tomatoes
4 spring onions, chopped
2 tbsp chopped fresh parsley
1 garlic clove, finely chopped
4 tbsp olive oil
1 tbsp lemon juice
650g/1lb 7oz new potatoes, halved
4 rashers unsmoked bacon
4 hard-boiled eggs
lettuce, to serve

Takes 30 minutes • Serves 4

1 Finely chop 225g/8oz of the tomatoes and combine with the spring onions, parsley, garlic, oil and lemon juice to make a salsa. Season to taste. Cook the new potatoes in lightly salted boiling water until just tender. Drain and refresh under cold running water. Thickly slice.

2 Preheat the grill to high and cook the bacon for 3–4 minutes until crisp. Allow to cool slightly then break into bite-sized pieces. Cut the remaining tomatoes and the eggs into eighths.

3 Toss the potatoes, egg, tomato slices and tomato salsa in a serving bowl. Season to taste. Scatter over the bacon and serve on a bed of lettuce.

• Per serving 362 kcalories, protein 14g, carbohydrate 32g, fat 21g, saturated fat 4g, fibre 4g, added sugar none, salt 1.05g

Cubed feta cheese sold in jars of olive oil is ideal for this recipe.
Use the oil to make the dressing.

Warm Chickpea Salad

1 red onion, cut into wedges
2 courgettes, thickly sliced
1 red pepper, seeded and
cut into large chunks
375g/13oz ripe tomatoes, halved
5 tbsp olive oil
juice of ½ a lemon
3 tbsp chopped fresh mixed herbs,
(chives, parsley and mint) or
3 tbsp chopped fresh parsley
2 × 400g cans chickpeas, drained
100g/4oz feta, cut into cubes
pitta bread, to serve

Takes 45 minutes • Serves 4

1 Preheat the oven to 220°C/Gas 7/fan oven 200°C. Put the onion, courgettes, red pepper and tomatoes into a shallow roasting tin and season with black pepper. Drizzle with two tablespoons of the olive oil and toss well. Roast for 30 minutes, stirring halfway through, until the vegetables are tender.
2 Meanwhile, mix together the lemon juice and remaining olive oil and season. Stir in the herbs.
3 Allow the vegetables to cool for 5 minutes, then tip into a bowl with the chickpeas, feta and lemon and olive oil dressing. Toss lightly before serving with pitta bread.

• Per serving 375 kcalories, protein 15g, carbohydrate 29g, fat 23g, saturated fat 5g, fibre 8g, added sugar none, salt 1.62g

Double Gloucester adds attractive
colour to the softened spinach.

Potato, Spinach and Cheese Melt

650g/1lb 7oz new potatoes,
cut into long wedges
1 tbsp oil
250g pack ready-washed
baby spinach leaves
100g/4oz Double Gloucester
1–2 tbsp snipped fresh chives
100g/4oz wafer-thin smoked ham

Takes 25 minutes • Serves 4

1 Bring a large pan of salted water to
the boil. Add the potatoes and boil for
12–15 minutes until tender.
2 Drain the potatoes well, then return to
the pan. Add the oil and lightly toss the
potatoes. Put the pan over a medium heat,
add the spinach, cover and shake the pan
occasionally until the spinach has wilted.
3 Cut the cheese into cubes or crumble
it straight into the pan. Season well and
add the chives. When the cheese starts
to melt, spoon on to hot serving plates.
Using scissors, snip strips of ham over the
top and serve straight away.

• Per serving 289 kcalories, protein 16g, carbohydrate
27g, fat 14g, saturated fat 6g, fibre 3g, added sugar
none, salt 1.31g

This salad looks most attractive when
you use Desirée or Romano potatoes.

Warm Potato and Broccoli Salad

700g/1lb 9oz potatoes,
cut into chunks
350g/12oz broccoli,
cut into florets
5 tbsp olive oil
1 onion, peeled and cut
into thin wedges
12 rashers rindless streaky bacon,
smoked or unsmoked
1 tbsp white wine vinegar
1 tbsp wholegrain mustard

Takes 40 minutes • Serves 4

1 Parboil the potatoes in salted boiling water
for 5 minutes, adding the broccoli for the last
3 minutes. Drain the potatoes and broccoli.
2 Heat two tablespoons of oil in a pan. Add
the onion and potatoes only and cook for
8–10 minutes until golden. Meanwhile, grill
the bacon until crisp, then drain on kitchen
paper. Add the broccoli to the pan with the
onion and potatoes and warm through. Tip
the vegetables into a bowl.
3 Add the remaining olive oil, vinegar and
mustard to the pan the onion was cooked in,
stirring until warm. Pour over the vegetables,
toss gently and season with pepper. Serve
with the bacon rashers on top.

• Per serving 492 kcalories, protein 19g, carbohydrate
34g, fat 32g, saturated fat 9g, fibre 5g, added sugar
none, salt 2.82g

A substantial main meal salad for all the
family to enjoy. It is good served warm or cold.

Ham, Potato and Feta Salad

1kg/2lb 4oz new potatoes,
halved if large
175g/6oz feta cheese cubes in oil
1 tsp dried oregano
8 tomatoes, roughly chopped
100g/4oz pitted black olives
225g/8oz (about 4 slices) thick-
sliced ham, cut into large pieces
handful of chopped fresh parsley

Takes 30 minutes • Serves 4

1 Bring a large pan of water to the boil (no
need to add salt). Add the potatoes and
cook for 15 minutes until tender.
2 Meanwhile, heat two tablespoons of
the feta oil in a pan. Add the oregano and
tomatoes and cook over a medium heat for
3–4 minutes, until slightly softened. Stir in
the olives, feta cubes and ham, and stir well.
Drain the potatoes and return to the pan.
3 Tip the olive and tomato mixture into the
potato pan and season. Sprinkle over the
parsley and toss lightly. Serve warm or cold.

• Per serving 408 kcalories, protein 23g, carbohydrate
47g, fat 16g, saturated fat 7g, fibre 5g, added sugar
none, salt 4.47g

Mix the ingredients, minus the avocado,
the night before eating for maximum flavour.

Salami, Bean and Avocado Salad

150g pack button
mushrooms, sliced
8 radishes, sliced
½ small red onion, thinly sliced
400g can haricot or cannellini
beans, drained
4 tbsp light olive oil
1 tbsp wine vinegar or cider vinegar
1 garlic clove, crushed
1 avocado
90g pack peppered salami, each
slice cut into eighths

Takes 15 minutes • Serves 4

1 In a bowl, toss the mushrooms, radishes, red onion and beans.
2 In a separate bowl, mix together the olive oil, vinegar and garlic. Season.
3 Peel and stone the avocado and cut the flesh into chunks. Gently stir into the bean mixture with the salami and the dressing. Check the seasoning and serve straight away.

• Per serving 362 kcalories, protein 11g, carbohydrate 14g, fat 29g, saturated fat 6g, fibre 6g, added sugar 2g, salt 1.24g

Cheese on toast for grown-ups,
but child's play to make.

Tomato Pizza Toasties

4 thick slices of bread
120g carton pesto sauce
8 tomatoes, weighing about
650g/1lb 7oz, thinly sliced
100g/4oz cheddar, grated

Takes 15 minutes • Serves 4

1 Preheat the grill to high. Toast the bread slices on one side. Turn over and spread a thin layer of pesto on the untoasted side.
2 Arrange the tomato slices over the top to cover. Season well.
3 Sprinkle over the cheese and grill for 5 minutes, until the cheese is golden and bubbling. Serve immediately.

• Per serving 380 kcalories, protein 17g, carbohydrate 25g, fat 24g, saturated fat 10g, fibre 2g, added sugar none, salt 1.36g

A quick and convenient storecupboard supper.
Be sure to use floury potatoes to keep the mix together.

Tuna, Onion and Sweetcorn Hash

750g/1lb 10oz floury potatoes, such
as King Edward, cut into chunks
bunch of spring onions, chopped
185g can tuna in brine, drained
100g/4oz frozen sweetcorn or
165g can sweetcorn, drained
2 tbsp oil
2 large tomatoes, sliced
85g/3oz cheddar, grated
baked beans or salad, to serve

Takes 25 minutes • Serves 4

1 Cook the potatoes in salted boiling water for 12–15 minutes until tender. Drain the potatoes, return to the pan and mash thoroughly. Stir in the spring onions, sweetcorn and tuna, and season well.
2 Preheat the grill to high. Heat the oil in a frying pan. Add the potato mixture, spreading it out in the pan, and fry over a medium heat for 4–5 minutes, until the underside is brown and crisp.
3 Arrange slices of tomato over the potato and sprinkle with the grated cheese. Grill until the top is golden and bubbling. Serve cut into wedges with baked beans or a salad.

• Per serving 387 kcalories, protein 21g, carbohydrate 39g, fat 17g, saturated fat 6g, fibre 4g, added sugar none, salt 0.69g

Kids will love these and
they're brilliant for barbecues too.

BLT Burgers

500g pack minced lamb,
pork or turkey
2 tbsp Worcestershire sauce
4 rashers smoked streaky bacon
tomato slices, lettuce leaves,
mayonnaise and 4 burger buns,
to serve

Takes 30 minutes • Serves 4

1 Preheat the grill to high, or light the barbecue. Season the mince well and stir in the Worcestershire sauce. Shape the mince into four burgers.
2 Cook the burgers under the grill or on the barbecue for 7–8 minutes on each side, until completely cooked through. Cook the bacon alongside the burgers for the last 8 minutes of cooking time, turning once, until crisp. Drain on kitchen paper.
3 Fill the buns with sliced tomatoes and lettuce leaves, then top with a burger. Lay a slice of bacon on top and finish with a spoonful of mayonnaise.

• Per serving 433 kcalories, protein 32g, carbohydrate 27g, fat 23g, saturated fat 10g, fibre 1g, added sugar none, salt 1.76g

*Chopped fresh apricots add juiciness and
a tangy flavour to pork mince.*

Pork and Apricot Burgers

500g packet pork mince
4 spring onions, finely chopped
4 tbsp chopped fresh mint
2 firm, fresh apricots, about
175g/6oz, roughly chopped
1 egg, beaten
200ml carton Greek yogurt
4 burger buns and lettuce leaves,
to serve

Takes 30 minutes • Serves 4

1 Mix together the pork mince, spring onions, two tablespoons of the mint and the apricots. Season well and bind together with the beaten egg. Divide the mixture into four, then shape each portion into 10cm/4in burgers.

2 Grill the burgers under a moderate heat or barbecue for 8–10 minutes on each side. While the burgers are cooking, mix together the Greek yogurt and remaining mint, then season.

3 Serve each burger in a bun with some lettuce, then spoon over the minty yogurt sauce. Serve the rest of the sauce separately.

• Per serving 300 kcalories, protein 30g, carbohydrate 5g, fat 18g, saturated fat 8g, fibre 1g, added sugar none, salt 0.35g

These kebabs make a lovely, lazy Sunday brunch. Prepare them the evening before, then next day just grill them and cook the rice.

Bacon Kebabs on Mushroom Rice

2 medium leeks, each cut into 4
4 flat mushrooms
14 rashers rindless streaky bacon, halved
4 herby sausages, halved vertically
300g/10oz long grain rice
50g/2oz butter, melted
1 tsp dried thyme
squeeze of lemon juice
200ml carton crème fraîche

Takes 35 minutes • Serves 4

1 Blanch the leeks in boiling water for 3–4 minutes, then drain. Chop one mushroom and the stems of all the mushrooms, and keep to one side. Cut the other mushrooms into quarters. Stretch the bacon with the back of a knife, then wrap around each piece of leek, mushroom quarter and sausage. Thread on to skewers.
2 Preheat the grill to high. Cook the rice. Melt half the butter with half the thyme and the lemon juice. Brush over the kebabs. Grill for 10 minutes, turning, until cooked.
3 Melt the remaining butter in a pan. Cook the reserved chopped mushrooms and remaining thyme until softened. Stir in the crème fraîche and season. Drain the rice and stir into the sauce. Stir the kebab pan juices into the rice. Serve immediately.

• Per serving 1023 kcalories, protein 27g, carbohydrate 73g, fat 71g, saturated fat 35g, fibre 1g, added sugar none, salt 4.72g

Mix the vegetables gently into the eggs so
they don't break up too much.

Pea, Ham and Potato Omelette

650g/1lb 7oz potatoes,
preferably red skinned, unpeeled
6 tbsp olive oil
1 onion, chopped
8 eggs
140g/5oz thick slice of ham, cubed
250g/9oz frozen peas

Takes 45 minutes • Serves 4

1 Thickly slice the potatoes. In a large frying pan, heat four tablespoons of the oil. Fry the potatoes gently for about 15 minutes, until beginning to turn golden and just tender. Add the onion to the pan and cook for 5 minutes.

2 In a large bowl, beat the eggs and season well. Tip the potatoes, onion, ham and peas into the beaten eggs. Mix gently so you don't break up the potatoes.

3 Preheat the grill to high. Heat the remaining oil in the pan. Add the egg mixture and cook gently for 10 minutes until half set, then grill for 10–15 minutes until the top of the omelette is golden and just set. Serve cut into wedges.

• Per serving 516 kcalories, protein 27g, carbohydrate 36g, fat 30g, saturated fat 6g, fibre 6g, added sugar none, salt 1.33g

An Italian-style omelette made from ingredients you're sure to have in your fridge.

Chunky Bacon and Cheese Frittata

8 rashers rindless back bacon
bunch of spring onions, sliced
8 large eggs
2 tbsp milk
85g/3oz cheddar, cut into
small cubes
knob of butter
tomato salsa and thick slices of
bread, to serve

Takes 35 minutes • Serves 4

1 Snip the bacon into small pieces. Cook in a non-stick frying pan for 5–6 minutes until the fat begins to run. Drain off some of the fat. Add the spring onions and cook for 5 minutes until tender and the bacon is crisp. Preheat the grill to medium.
2 Beat the eggs and milk together and add pepper. Reserve a little bacon and mix the rest into the eggs with the spring onions and cheese. Melt the butter in a 23cm/9in frying pan. Pour in the mixture and cook gently, without stirring, for 5–8 minutes until lightly set. Scatter over the reserved bacon.
3 Slide the pan under the grill to brown the top. Cut into wedges and serve with a chunky tomato salsa and bread.

• Per serving 468 kcalories, protein 31g, carbohydrate 2g, fat 38g, saturated fat 16g, fibre 1g, added sugar none, salt 3.21g

You can bake the potatoes in the microwave for 20 minutes first, but cook the eggs in the oven.

Baked Potatoes with Cracked Eggs

4 large baking potatoes (about 450g/1lb each in weight)
25g/1oz butter
140g/5oz broccoli, cut into small florets
100g/4oz mushrooms, sliced
8 medium eggs

Takes 1½ hours • Serves 4

1 Preheat the oven to 200°C/Gas 6/fan oven 180°C from cold. Bake the potatoes for 1–1¼ hours until they are cooked through and the skins are crisp. About 5 minutes before the end of the potatoes' cooking time, melt the butter in a frying pan. Add the broccoli and mushrooms and cook, stirring, for about 3 minutes, then set aside.

2 When the potatoes are cooked, cut each in half and scoop most of the flesh into a bowl. Stir in the broccoli, mushrooms and pan juices. Season well. Spoon back into the potato skins and make a well in the middle. Set the potatoes on a baking tray.

3 Carefully crack an egg into each well. (Don't worry if the egg white spills over a little.) Return to the oven and cook for 15 minutes until the eggs have just set.

• Per serving 358 kcalories, protein 19g, carbohydrate 35g, fat 17g, saturated fat 6g, fibre 4g, added sugar none, salt 0.52g

Choose large floury potatoes, such as King Edward or Maris Piper and serve for a light lunch or supper.

Cheesy Potato Jackets

4 baking potatoes, about 350g/12oz each in weight, scrubbed
50g/2oz butter
4 tbsp milk
100g/4oz cheddar, grated
2 eggs, beaten
splash of Tabasco

Takes 1½ hours • Serves 4

1 Preheat the oven to 200°C/Gas 6/fan oven 180°C from cold. Rub the potatoes with a little salt, then transfer to a baking sheet and cook for 1–1¼ hours, until tender. Remove from the oven and leave until cool enough to handle.

2 Using a sharp knife, cut the tops off the potatoes and scoop the insides into a bowl, leaving the shells intact. Mash the potato flesh with a fork, beat in the butter, milk, 85g/3oz of the cheese, the eggs and Tabasco. Season. Pile back into the potato shells.

3 Scatter the remaining cheese over the top and bake for a further 20 minutes, until fluffy and golden.

• Per serving 509 kcalories, protein 18g, carbohydrate 61.1g, fat 23g, saturated fat 13.1g fibre 4.6g, added sugar none, salt 0.89g

*Huge tomatoes make tasty containers for
a scrumptious stuffing.*

Corn Stuffed Tomatoes

4 large beef tomatoes
sprinkling of caster sugar
2 tbsp olive oil
1 leek, thinly sliced
4 rashers streaky bacon, chopped
½ tbsp chopped fresh rosemary
3 slices day-old white bread
85g/3oz frozen or canned sweetcorn
175g/6oz gruyère, diced
2 tbsp chopped fresh parsley

Takes 45 minutes • Serves 4

1 Preheat the oven to 200°C/Gas 6/fan oven 180°C. Cut the tops off the tomatoes and discard. Using a spoon, scoop out the seeds to leave a hollow shell. Lightly season inside with a little sugar, salt and pepper, then put in a greased shallow baking dish.
2 Heat the oil in a frying pan and cook the leek, bacon and rosemary for 7 minutes, stirring occasionally. Meanwhile, cut the bread into cubes, then cook in the pan for 3 minutes, stirring to brown all over. Season, then add the corn, cheese and parsley.
3 Divide the stuffing between the tomatoes and bake for 20 minutes until the filling is golden.

• Per serving 321 kcalories, protein 15g, carbohydrate 22g, fat 20g, saturated fat 8g, fibre 3g, added sugar none, salt 1.46g

Cheesy, herby choux pastry puffs are good with
tomato sauce or with smoked haddock.

Herbed Cheese Puff

70g/2½oz plain flour
pinch of English mustard powder
50g/2oz butter, cubed
100g/4oz mature cheddar, grated
2 eggs, beaten
3 tbsp chopped fresh mixed herbs
steamed broccoli or leeks, to serve

FOR THE TOMATO SAUCE
1 tbsp olive oil
1 garlic clove, chopped or crushed
400g can tomatoes
1 tbsp tomato purée

Takes 50 minutes • Serves 4

1 Preheat the oven to 220°C/Gas 7/fan
oven 200°C. Grease a baking sheet. Sift
the flour, mustard powder and a pinch of salt
on to a sheet of greaseproof paper. Bring the
butter and 150ml/¼ pint water to the boil. Tip
in the flour, remove from the heat and beat to
a smooth thick paste. Beat in 85g/3oz of the
cheese. Leave to cool for 5 minutes.
2 Gradually beat the eggs into the paste,
then stir in the herbs. Drop spoonfuls on to
the baking sheet spaced slightly apart, to
form a 20cm/8in ring. Sprinkle over the
remaining cheese.
3 Bake for 25–30 minutes until puffed up
and crisp. Meanwhile, put the tomato sauce
ingredients in a small pan. Season. Bring to
the boil, stirring, then simmer for 10 minutes
until thickened. Cut the puff into wedges.
Serve with the sauce and broccoli or leeks.

• Per serving 340 kcalories, protein 13g, carbohydrate
18g, fat 25g, saturated fat 13g, fibre 2g, added sugar
none, salt 0.88g

Choose a mild soft cheese that doesn't overpower the flavour of the tomatoes.

Goat's Cheese and Tomato Tart

1 medium floury potato, peeled
85g/3oz cold butter, cut into pieces
1 onion, finely chopped
7 fresh thyme sprigs or 1 tsp dried
140g/5oz plain flour
450g/1lb ripe tomatoes,
thickly sliced
1 tbsp red wine vinegar
100g/4oz soft goat's cheese
olive oil, for drizzling
green salad, to serve

Takes 55 minutes • Serves 4

1 Preheat the oven to 200°C/Gas 6/fan oven 180°C. Chop the potatoes, then cook in salted boiling water for 10–12 minutes. Drain and mash. Meanwhile, melt 25g/1oz butter in a small pan and cook the onion until beginning to brown. Strip the leaves from four thyme sprigs and add to the pan, or add half the dried thyme.

2 In a bowl, rub the remaining butter into the flour. Add the onion, pan juices and mashed potatoes, and season. Mix to a soft dough, then press into a 23cm/9in round on a greased baking sheet.

3 Arrange the tomatoes on the dough and drizzle over the vinegar. Sprinkle over the remaining thyme and season. Crumble the cheese over and drizzle with oil. Bake for 35–40 minutes. Serve with a green salad.

• Per serving 434 kcalories, protein 11g, carbohydrate 39g, fat 27g, saturated fat 16g, fibre 3g, added sugar none, salt 0.89g

Use your microwave to speed up
the baking of the potatoes.

Jackets with Leeks and Mackerel

4 large baking potatoes
50g/2oz butter
2 large leeks (about 500g/1lb 2oz),
thinly sliced
2 tbsp creamed horseradish
3 smoked mackerel fillets,
skinned and flaked
squeeze of fresh lemon juice

Takes 1 hour 10 minutes • Serves 4

1 Preheat the oven to 200°C/Gas 6/fan oven 180°C from cold. Bake the potatoes for about 1¼ hours, until crisp on the outside and tender all the way through.
2 When the potatoes are almost done, heat half the butter in a pan. Cook the leeks for about 6 minutes until softened, stirring regularly. Add the horseradish, flaked mackerel and lemon juice, and season.
3 Halve the baked potatoes and fluff up the flesh with a fork. Pile the leek and fish mixture on top, dot with the remaining butter and serve hot.

• Per serving 619 kcalories, protein 24g, carbohydrate 44g, fat 40g, saturated fat 13g, fibre 6g, added sugar none, salt 2.17g

Use packets of pizza-base mix to keep
preparation to a minimum.

Tuna Pizza Squares

2 × 145g packets pizza-base mix
2 tbsp olive oil, plus extra
for brushing
2 onions, thinly sliced
200g can chopped tomatoes
½ tsp dried oregano
200g can tuna, drained
85g/3oz stoned black olives
50g/2oz cheddar, grated
green salad, to serve

Takes 35 minutes • Serves 4

1 Grease a 33 × 28cm/13 × 11in Swiss
roll tin. Put the pizza-base mixes in a bowl,
add 250ml/9fl oz warm water and mix
together to make a smooth dough. Knead
for 5 minutes, then roll out on to a floured
surface to the same size as the tin. Put the
dough in the tin and brush with olive oil.
2 Preheat the oven to 200°C/Gas 6/fan
oven 180°C. Heat the oil in a frying pan
and fry the onions until golden. Set aside.
Spread the tomatoes on to the dough base.
Scatter over the oregano and season.
3 Break the tuna into chunks and arrange
on the base with the olives. Scatter the
onions and cheese on top and bake for
15–20 minutes, until the dough is risen,
golden and cooked through. Cut into
squares and serve with a salad.

• Per serving 633 kcalories, protein 28g, carbohydrate
91g, fat 18g, saturated fat 5g, fibre 6g, added sugar
3g, salt 3.52g

Ready-made puff pastry and cheese sauce
make this quick to assemble.

Spinach and Ham Tart

250g/9oz frozen leaf spinach
2 eggs
300g carton ready-made
cheese sauce
150ml/¼ pint milk
225g/8oz wafer-thin ham
375g sheet ready-rolled puff pastry,
thawed if frozen

Takes 40 minutes • Serves 6

1 Preheat the oven to 200°C/Gas 6/fan oven 180°C. Thaw the spinach in the microwave for 8 minutes on defrost. Pat really dry with kitchen paper. Beat the eggs into the cheese sauce with the milk and some freshly ground black pepper. Roughly tear each ham slice in half.
2 Unroll the pastry and roll it out a bit more to line a 35 × 23cm/14 × 9in Swiss roll tin. Scatter the spinach over the pastry base, then the ham in rough folds. Pour over the cheese sauce mixture.
3 Bake the tart for 25–30 minutes until set and golden on top.

• Per serving 414 kcalories, protein 18g, carbohydrate 30g, fat 26g, saturated fat 5g, fibre 1g, added sugar none, salt 2.21g

If you find anchovies a bit too salty,
rinse them in milk before adding them.

Pepperoni Pizza Tart

250g/9oz ready-made shortcrust pastry
3 tbsp olive oil
450g/1lb onions, thinly sliced
2 garlic cloves, crushed
2 x 425g cans chopped tomatoes, drained
1 tsp dried oregano
25g/1oz thinly sliced pepperoni
85g/3oz mature cheddar, grated
50g can anchovy fillets in oil, drained and halved lengthways
12 black olives
salad, to serve

Takes 1¼ hours • Serves 6

1 Roll out the pastry and line a 23cm/9in flan tin. Chill while you make the filling. Heat the oil in a pan and fry the onions and garlic for 15 minutes until soft. Cool for 10 minutes, then spread over the pastry.
2 Preheat the oven to 220°C/Gas 7/fan oven 200°C. Spread the tomatoes over the onions, sprinkle with oregano and top with the pepperoni. Sprinkle over the cheese and arrange the anchovies and olives on top.
3 Bake for 25–30 minutes until the pastry is cooked. Serve hot or cold with a salad.

• Per serving 376 kcalories, protein 10g, carbohydrate 28g, fat 25g, saturated fat 10g, fibre 4g, added sugar none, salt 1.68g

You can make one big cake by pressing
the mix into a frying pan instead. Grill the top.

Bubble and Squeak Cakes

700g/1lb 9oz floury potatoes, such
as Maris Piper, cut into chunks
4 carrots, sliced
350g/12oz green
cabbage, shredded
50g/2oz cheddar, grated
175g/6oz thick slice of ham, cubed
1 bunch spring onions, finely sliced
1–2 tbsp wholegrain mustard
25g/1oz butter
2 tbsp oil

FOR THE SAUCE
400g can chopped tomatoes
1 tbsp tomato purée
1 tsp sugar

Takes 40 minutes, plus chilling •
Serves 4

1 Cook the potatoes and carrots in salted
water for 15 minutes until tender. Steam the
cabbage over the pan for 8 minutes. Drain
well. Return the potatoes and carrots to the
pan and mash.
2 Stir in the cabbage, cheese, ham, half
the spring onions and mustard to taste.
Divide the mixture into eight and shape
into 10cm/4in cakes. Chill for 30 minutes.
To make the sauce, cook the tomatoes,
remaining spring onions, purée, sugar and
seasoning for 10 minutes.
3 Heat half the butter and oil in a frying pan.
Fry four cakes at a time for 3–4 minutes on
each side until golden. Keep them warm
while frying the others in the rest of the
butter and oil. Serve with the sauce.

• Per serving 423 kcalories, protein 21g, carbohydrate
45g, fat 19g, saturated fat 8g, fibre 9g, added sugar
1g, salt 2.03g

This contemporary variation on traditional fresh
pesto sauce is made from watercress, walnuts and lime.

Fettucine with Watercress Pesto

350g/12oz fettucine
85g/3oz watercress
100g/4oz walnuts, chopped
50g/2oz parmesan, grated
1 garlic clove
finely grated zest and
juice of 2 limes
100ml/3½fl oz olive oil
Italian bread and tomato salad,
to serve

Takes 15 minutes • Serves 4

1 Cook the pasta in lightly salted boiling
water according to the packet instructions.
2 Meanwhile, put the watercress, half the
walnuts, the parmesan, garlic and lime zest
and juice in a food processor and whizz to a
paste. With the motor still running, gradually
drizzle in the olive oil. Season.
3 Drain the pasta and return to the pan. Stir
in the pesto, then divide the pasta between
serving bowls. Scatter over the remaining
walnuts and serve with Italian bread and a
tomato salad.

• Per serving 763 kcalories, protein 20g, carbohydrate
67g, fat 48g, saturated fat 8g, fibre 4g, added sugar
none, salt 0.42g

Ring the changes by using blue cheese,
or for non-veggies, top with strips of crispy bacon.

Spaghetti with Tomato and Brie

300g/10oz spaghetti
500g/1lb 2oz courgettes,
halved lengthways
3 tbsp olive oil
2 garlic cloves, thinly sliced
finely grated zest and
juice of 1 lemon
6 ripe tomatoes, roughly chopped
140g/5oz brie, diced

Takes 35 minutes • Serves 4

1 Cook the spaghetti in salted boiling water for 10–12 minutes until tender or according to the packet instructions. Meanwhile, slice the courgettes. Heat the oil in a large frying pan, then fry the courgettes and garlic for 3–4 minutes until softened.
2 Add the lemon zest, tomatoes and about three tablespoons of the pasta water (enough to make a sauce). Cook for a further 2–3 minutes until the tomatoes begin to soften. Remove from the heat and stir in the brie so it just starts to melt. Season and add lemon juice to taste.
3 Drain the spaghetti well and add to the tomato sauce mixture. Toss well together, divide between bowls and serve.

• Per serving 490 kcalories, protein 19g, carbohydrate 62g, fat 20g, saturated fat 7g, fibre 5g, added sugar none, salt 0.66g

Roasting the vegetables makes them sweet-tasting, rich and satisfying.

Roasted Vegetable Pasta

2 courgettes, cut into sticks
1 red pepper, seeded and
cut into strips
2 garlic cloves, finely sliced
3 tbsp olive oil
300g/10oz pasta shells
200ml carton half-fat crème fraîche
2 tsp wholegrain mustard
85g/3oz cheddar, grated

Takes 30 minutes • Serves 4

1 Preheat the oven to 220°C/Gas 7/fan oven 200°C. Put the courgettes and red pepper in a roasting tin and sprinkle over the sliced garlic.
2 Drizzle with olive oil, then season and toss to make sure all the vegetables are coated with oil. Roast for 15–20 minutes, until the vegetables are tender and just beginning to brown.
3 Bring a large pan of salted water to the boil. Add the pasta and cook for 10–12 minutes until just cooked. Drain, then stir into the roasted vegetables with the crème fraîche, mustard and grated cheddar. Serve immediately.

• Per serving 490 kcalories, protein 19g, carbohydrate 62g, fat 20g, saturated fat 9g, fibre 4g, added sugar none, salt 0.58g

A quick supper made mostly from storecupboard ingredients.

Mushroom and Tuna Spaghetti

350g/12oz spaghetti

FOR THE SAUCE
2 tbsp olive oil
1 garlic clove, chopped
175g/6oz mushrooms, sliced
cupful of frozen peas
200g can tuna in brine, drained
200ml carton half-fat crème fraîche
2 tbsp lemon juice

Takes 20 minutes • Serves 4

1 Cook the spaghetti in a large pan of salted boiling water for 10–12 minutes, until just tender.

2 Meanwhile, make the sauce. Heat the oil in a pan, then fry the garlic and mushrooms over a high heat for about 3 minutes, until the mushrooms start to soften. Add the peas and cook for a further 2 minutes, stirring. Flake the tuna into the pan, then add the crème fraîche and lemon juice, and season. Heat through gently.

3 Drain the pasta and return to the pan. Stir in the sauce and mix well. Serve on warmed plates with a grinding of pepper.

• Per serving 516 kcalories, protein 26g, carbohydrate 73g, fat 16g, saturated fat 6g, fibre 6g, added sugar none, salt 0.72g

Look for smoked-salmon trimmings
to keep costs down.

Tagliatelle with Smoked Salmon

1 tbsp vegetable oil
250g/9oz chestnut or button
mushrooms, quartered
375g/13oz dried or fresh tagliatelle
125g pack smoked salmon
(trimmings are fine), chopped
3 tbsp chopped fresh parsley
200ml carton half-fat crème fraîche
juice of ½ lemon
salad, to serve

Takes 20 minutes • Serves 4

1 Heat the oil in a frying pan. Add the mushrooms and cook for 8 minutes until beginning to brown.
2 Meanwhile, bring a large pan of salted water to the boil. Add the pasta and cook according to the packet instructions.
3 Stir the salmon, parsley, crème fraîche and lemon juice into the mushrooms and season. Drain the pasta and quickly toss with the creamy sauce. Serve immediately with a salad.

• Per serving 484 kcalories, protein 22g, carbohydrate 72g, fat 14g, saturated fat 6g, fibre 4g, added sugar none, salt 1.64g

Try adding pitted black olives or rinsed,
drained capers to this dish just before serving.

Tuna and Two Cheese Pasta

300g/10oz penne
350g/12oz broccoli florets
250g carton cottage cheese
with chives
140g/5oz mature cheddar, grated
200g can tuna in brine, drained

Takes 20 minutes • Serves 4

1 Cook the pasta in a large pan of salted boiling water for 10–12 minutes until just tender, adding the broccoli florets to the pan for the last 3–4 minutes of cooking.
2 Drain the pasta and broccoli, then return to the hot pan. Gently stir in the cottage cheese and cheddar so it melts into the pasta.
3 Carefully mix in the chunks of tuna, trying not to break them up too much. Season and serve.

• Per serving 533 kcalories, protein 40g, carbohydrate 60g, fat 17g, saturated fat 9g, fibre 5g, added sugar none, salt 1.54g

Roast the tomatoes to emphasise their
sweetness and concentrate the flavour.

Tomato and Salmon Pasta

2 tbsp fresh oregano leaves,
or 1 tsp dried
900g/2lb small ripe tomatoes
2 onions, sliced
1 garlic clove, finely chopped
2 tbsp olive oil
350g/12oz spaghetti
450g/1lb boneless skinless
salmon fillet
garlic bread, to serve

Takes 40 minutes • Serves 4

1 Preheat the oven to 200°C/Gas 6/fan oven 180°C. If using fresh oregano, strip the leaves from the stems. Tip half the oregano leaves, or all the dried oregano, into a roasting tin with the tomatoes, onions and garlic. Drizzle over the oil. Season, then stir well. Roast for 30 minutes, stirring occasionally, until the tomatoes have softened.
2 Cook the spaghetti in salted boiling water for 10–12 minutes, stirring occasionally. Meanwhile, cut the salmon into bite-sized cubes. Add to the roasting tin for the last 5 minutes of cooking time.
3 Drain the pasta and spoon into the tomatoes and salmon. Sprinkle over the remaining fresh oregano, if using, and serve hot with garlic bread.

• Per serving 615 kcalories, protein 36g, carbohydrate 77g, fat 20g, saturated fat 4g, fibre 6g, added sugar none, salt 0.19g

Ready-made stock (fresh or in cubes) can be quite salty,
so don't season this dish until the sauce is cooked.

Minted Chicken Rigatoni

350g/12oz rigatoni
225g/8oz fresh or frozen peas
knob of butter
1 tbsp vegetable oil
1 red pepper, seeded and sliced
4 boneless skinless chicken breasts,
cut into 2.5cm/1in cubes
1 onion, finely chopped
1 garlic clove, finely chopped
200ml/7fl oz chicken stock
4 tbsp chopped fresh mint, plus a
few leaves to garnish
1 tbsp wholegrain mustard
200ml carton crème fraîche

Takes 35 minutes • Serves 4

1 Cook the pasta in salted boiling water
for 10–12 minutes, adding the peas for the
last 3 minutes.
2 Heat the butter and oil in a large frying
pan. Add the red pepper and cook for
5 minutes until starting to brown. Transfer to
a plate. Add the chicken and onion to the
pan and cook over a high heat for 8 minutes,
until the chicken is browned. Stir in the garlic
for the last minute.
3 Add the stock, bring to the boil, then
cook for 3 minutes to reduce by half. Stir in
the red pepper, mint, mustard and crème
fraîche. Season with pepper – add salt if
necessary. Drain the pasta, stir into the
chicken and serve.

• Per serving 718 kcalories, protein 51g, carbohydrate
80g, fat 23.8g, saturated fat 11.8g fibre 6.3g, added
sugar none, salt 0.72g

You can use this all-in-one method
of sauce-making in other recipes too.

Chicken and Spinach Pasta

350g/12oz pasta, such as penne
175g/6oz frozen leaf spinach
1 tbsp oil
4 boneless skinless chicken thighs,
cut into strips
1 garlic clove, finely chopped
425ml/¾ pint semi-skimmed milk
25g/1oz plain flour
25g/1oz butter
140g/5oz mature cheddar, grated
freshly grated nutmeg, to taste

Takes 50 minutes • Serves 4

1 Cook the pasta in salted boiling water for 10 minutes, adding the spinach for the last 3–4 minutes of cooking time. Drain well. Meanwhile, heat the oil in a wok or large pan, add the chicken strips and garlic and stir fry for 3–4 minutes, until the meat is well browned and cooked through. Remove from the pan and set aside.
2 Add the milk to the pan, sprinkle in the flour, then add the butter and whisk over a medium heat until thickened and smooth. Stir in about 85g/3oz of the cheese and season with salt, pepper and nutmeg.
3 Preheat the grill to high. Mix the chicken into the sauce with the pasta and spinach. Spoon into an ovenproof dish, sprinkle with the remaining cheese and grill until golden.

• Per serving 705 kcalories, protein 44g, carbohydrate 78g, fat 27g, saturated fat 13g, fibre 4g, added sugar none, salt 1.11g

*Soft cheese with herbs and garlic makes
an almost instant pasta sauce.*

Herby Pasta with Peas and Bacon

350g/12oz pasta, such as penne
350g/12oz frozen peas
1 large red pepper, seeded and
cut into chunks
8 rashers rindless streaky bacon
150g pack soft cheese with herbs
and garlic
300ml/½ pint milk

Takes 20 minutes • Serves 4

1 Cook the pasta according to the packet instructions. About 5 minutes before the end of the cooking time, add the frozen peas and red pepper. Bring back to the boil and cook for 5 minutes.

2 Meanwhile, preheat the grill to high and grill the bacon until crispy. Snip into bite-sized pieces.

3 Put the soft cheese and milk into a large saucepan. Warm through, stirring continuously until smooth and thickened. Drain the pasta and vegetables, and toss with the cheese sauce and bacon. Season with freshly ground black pepper.

• Per serving 686 kcalories, protein 26g, carbohydrate 81g, fat 31g, saturated fat 16g, fibre 8g, added sugar none, salt 1.71g

A cheap and easy supper made from
readily available ingredients.

Leek, Pea and Ham Pasta

300g/10oz spaghetti
175g/6oz frozen peas
25g/1oz butter
1 large leek
4 eggs
140g/5oz thick slice of smoked
ham, cut into cubes
85g/3oz cheddar or Lancashire
cheese, grated

Takes 15 minutes • Serves 4

1 Bring a large pan of salted water to the boil. Add the spaghetti and cook for about 10–12 minutes, adding the peas for the last 3 minutes of the cooking time.
2 Meanwhile, heat the butter in a small pan. Wash and slice the leek. Add to the pan and cook over a medium heat for 3 minutes until softened.
3 Beat the eggs in a bowl and season. Drain the pasta and immediately return to the pan. Tip in the leeks, eggs, ham and half the cheese. Stir well. Adjust the seasoning and serve sprinkled with the remaining cheese.

• Per serving 553 kcalories, protein 32g, carbohydrate 61g, fat 22g, saturated fat 10g, fibre 6g, added sugar none, salt 1:67g

Bacon, garlic and herbs added to Toulouse sausages
give this sauce plenty of extra flavour.

Sausage and Tomato Spaghetti

1 tbsp olive oil
1 onion, chopped
450g/1lb Toulouse or
herby sausages
400g can chopped tomatoes
1 bay leaf
pinch of sugar
350g/12oz spaghetti
2 courgettes, cut into 5cm/2in sticks
50g/2oz grated parmesan or
mature cheddar

Takes 45 minutes • Serves 4

1 Heat the oil in a pan, then fry the onion for 8 minutes, stirring occasionally, until golden. Remove the skins from the sausages and discard. Add the sausages to the pan and cook for 10 minutes until they start to brown, breaking them up with a spatula.
2 Add the tomatoes, bay leaf and a pinch of sugar, and season. Bring to the boil, cover and simmer for 15 minutes until cooked.
3 Meanwhile, cook the spaghetti in salted boiling water for 10–12 minutes until tender, adding the courgettes for the last 5 minutes of the cooking time. Drain, then stir into the sausage sauce with half the cheese. Serve hot with the remaining cheese sprinkled over.

• Per serving 690 kcalories, protein 33g, carbohydrate 78g, fat 30g, saturated fat 11g, fibre 4g, added sugar 1g, salt 2.92g

Try a change from your usual sausage.
Most supermarkets stock some exotic varieties.

Spicy Sausage Pasta

2 tbsp olive oil
6 good-quality sausages
1 onion, finely chopped
1 garlic clove, chopped
400g can chopped tomatoes
1 tsp dried oregano
350g/12oz penne or rigatoni pasta
1 tbsp red pesto

Takes 35 minutes • Serves 4

1 Heat the oil in a frying pan and cook the sausages over a high heat for about 8 minutes until brown. Remove from the pan and cut into 2.5cm/1in pieces.
2 Fry the onion and garlic in the frying pan for 5 minutes. Add the tomatoes, sausage pieces and oregano, and season to taste. Cover, reduce the heat and simmer for 10 minutes. Meanwhile, cook the pasta in salted boiling water for 10–12 minutes until just tender.
3 When the sauce has thickened, stir in the pesto. Drain the pasta and return to the pan. Stir in the sauce and serve immediately.

• Per serving 652 kcalories, protein 27g, carbohydrate 77g, fat 29g, saturated fat 8g, fibre 4g, added sugar none, salt 2.17g

Make double the amount of meatballs
and sauce and freeze half for later.

Spicy Spaghetti with Meatballs

15g packet mixed fresh
Mediterranean herbs
(basil, oregano and parsley) –
leaves stripped from their stalks
500g packet pork mince
1 egg, beaten
25g/1oz fresh breadcrumbs
2 garlic cloves, crushed
2 large onions, finely chopped
2 tbsp oil
2 tbsp tomato purée
1kg/2lb 4oz ripe tomatoes, chopped
½ tsp sugar
1 tbsp Dijon mustard
350g/12oz spaghetti

Takes 1 hour 10 minutes • Serves 4

1 Chop the parsley and basil, mix with
the mince, egg, breadcrumbs, garlic and
half the chopped onion, then season. Shape
into 20 balls. Heat the oil in a large frying
pan. Fry the meatballs for 4–5 minutes,
turning frequently, until browned, then
remove from the pan.
2 Fry the remaining onion until golden.
Add the tomato purée, tomatoes, sugar,
425ml/¾ pint water and half the oregano.
Simmer for 5 minutes. Whizz in a food
processor until smooth. Return to the pan.
3 Add the mustard and meatballs. Simmer,
for 25 minutes, then season. Meanwhile,
cook and drain the spaghetti. Divide between
serving bowls and add the meatballs and
sauce. Sprinkle with the remaining oregano.

• Per serving 689 kcalories, protein 41g, carbohydrate
88g, fat 22g, saturated fat 6g, fibre 7g, added sugar
1g, salt 0.77g

Quick-cook noodles with a peanut dressing
are topped with tender pork escalopes.

Peanut Noodles with Pork

250g packet medium egg noodles
2 tbsp olive oil, plus extra
for greasing
4 pork escalopes
50g/2oz salted peanuts
2 tbsp dark soy sauce
1 garlic clove, finely chopped
bunch of spring onions, sliced
100g/4oz beansprouts

Takes 25 minutes • Serves 4

1 Boil the noodles according to the packet instructions. Meanwhile, heat a griddle pan and brush with a little oil. Season the escalopes, then griddle for 2–3 minutes on each side until cooked through. Keep hot.
2 Put the peanuts in a plastic food bag and crush roughly with a rolling pin. Drain the noodles.
3 Mix together the olive oil, soy sauce and garlic, then toss with the noodles, spring onions, beansprouts and peanuts, and season with black pepper. Divide the noodles between four plates and top with the pork.

• Per serving 581 kcalories, protein 45g, carbohydrate 49g, fat 24g, saturated fat 4g, fibre 2g, added sugar none, salt 2.02g

Make the most of quick-cooking ingredients to create an appetising stir fry. For vegetarians, replace the pork with mushrooms.

Pork and Ginger Noodles

2 tbsp sunflower oil
450g/1lb pork fillet, cut into thin strips about 1cm/½in wide
2.5cm/1in piece fresh root ginger, grated
2 garlic cloves, finely chopped
½ savoy cabbage, about 250g/9oz, shredded
300ml/½ pint vegetable or chicken stock
1 tbsp soy sauce
100g/4oz frozen peas
2 × 150g packets Straight-to-Wok noodles
2 tbsp chopped fresh coriander, to serve

Takes 25 minutes • Serves 4

1 Heat the oil in a wok over a high heat, add the pork and stir fry for 3–4 minutes until just cooked. Stir in the ginger and garlic and continue to fry for 1–2 minutes.
2 Add the cabbage and stir fry with the pork until well combined. Pour over the stock and soy sauce.
3 Add the peas and noodles, stir well, then simmer for 5 minutes, until the cabbage is cooked but still crunchy. Scatter with coriander and serve.

• Per serving 337 kcalories, protein 31g, carbohydrate 28g, fat 12g, saturated fat 2g, fibre 4g, added sugar none, salt 1.84g

Make extra marinade and keep chilled,
ready to add a kick to your cooking.

Piri Piri Chicken

2 red chillies
1 red pepper
3 tbsp red wine vinegar
4 tbsp olive oil
4 boneless chicken breasts (skin on)
salad leaves, to serve

Takes 30 minutes, plus marinating •
Serves 4 (easily doubled)

1 Halve and seed the chillies and red pepper. Chop the chillies finely and the pepper roughly. Tip into a food processor and add the vinegar and oil, and season. Whizz, but leave chunky.

2 Slash the chicken breasts across the skin side and put in a shallow ovenproof dish. Pour over three-quarters of the marinade, turning the chicken to coat it. Marinate for at least 10 minutes, or overnight in the fridge if you have time. Reserve the remaining marinade.

3 Heat a griddle or heavy frying pan, add the chicken and cook for 5–6 minutes each side, turning once. Serve on a bed of salad leaves with the reserved marinade drizzled over.

• Per serving 393 kcalories, protein 27g, carbohydrate 3g, fat 30g, saturated fat 7g, fibre 1g, added sugar none, salt 0.26g

A complete meal, with tender
chicken and warm new potatoes.

Griddled Chicken Salad

450g/1lb new potatoes, halved
4 boneless skinless chicken breasts
5 tbsp olive oil
juice of 1 lemon
handful of fresh chives,
finely snipped
4 tbsp soured cream
1 cos or romaine lettuce, shredded
250g/9oz cherry tomatoes, halved

Takes 50 minutes • Serves 4

1 Cook the potatoes in salted boiling water
for 15–20 minutes until tender. Meanwhile,
flatten the chicken between two sheets
of cling film with a rolling pin, and then
season. In a large bowl, mix together the
olive oil, lemon juice and chives. Brush a
third of the dressing over the chicken.
2 Heat a griddle or large frying pan. Cook
the chicken for 6–8 minutes, turning halfway.
(You may need to do this in batches.)
Whisk the soured cream into the remaining
dressing and season.
3 Drain the potatoes and leave to cool slightly,
then toss with another third of the dressing.
Dress the lettuce and tomatoes with half the
remaining dressing. Divide between plates
with the potatoes. Top with the chicken and
drizzle over the remaining dressing.

• Per serving 412 kcalories, protein 37g, carbohydrate
22g, fat 20g, saturated fat 5g, fibre 2g, added sugar
none, salt 0.29g

Substitute the chicken stock with the
same amount of dry white wine or cider if you like.

Chicken with Cannellini Beans

2 tbsp olive oil
4 boneless chicken breasts,
skin left on
½ tsp paprika
1 small onion, finely chopped
100g/4oz bacon, finely chopped
230g can chopped tomatoes
400g can cannellini beans, drained
150ml/¼ pint chicken stock
squeeze of lemon juice
2 tbsp chopped fresh parsley

Takes 35 minutes • Serves 4

1 Heat the oil in a large frying pan. Season the chicken and sprinkle with paprika. Fry, skin-side down, for 8–10 minutes until the skin is golden and crispy. Turn and cook for a further 5–6 minutes until the chicken is cooked. Remove the chicken and keep warm.
2 Add the onion and bacon to the pan and cook for 5 minutes, stirring until the onion is cooked and the bacon is crispy.
3 Tip in the tomatoes, beans and stock. Stir well, then return the chicken to the pan. Bring to the boil, then reduce the heat and simmer for 2–3 minutes. Season, then stir in a squeeze of lemon juice. Sprinkle over the parsley. Serve straight from the pan.

• Per serving 455 kcalories, protein 38g, carbohydrate 15g, fat 27g, saturated fat 7g, fibre 5g, added sugar 2g, salt 1.52g

You can't beat fresh tarragon but frozen,
available in supermarkets, will do.

Chicken and Tarragon Dauphinoise

900g/2lb floury potatoes, such as
Maris Piper or King Edward
1 tbsp oil
25g/1oz butter
1 small onion, finely chopped
450g/1lb boneless skinless chicken
breasts, cut into 1cm/½in strips
1 tbsp chopped fresh tarragon
200ml carton crème fraîche
175g/6oz gruyère, grated
green salad, to serve

Takes 55 minutes • Serves 4
(easily doubled)

1 Preheat the oven to 200°C/Gas 6/fan
oven 180°C from cold. Butter a shallow
ovenproof dish. Slice the potatoes thinly and
cook in salted boiling water for 10 minutes
until just tender. Drain well.
2 Meanwhile, heat the oil and butter.
Fry the onion for 5 minutes until softened.
Add the chicken and fry over a high heat
until nicely browned. Lower the heat, stir
in the tarragon and half the crème fraîche,
then season well.
3 Spread half the potatoes in the dish.
Spoon over the chicken mixture and
cover with the remaining potatoes. Dot
spoonfuls of the remaining crème fraîche
on top and sprinkle with gruyère. Bake for
20–25 minutes until crisp and golden. Serve
with a green salad.

• Per serving 700 kcalories, protein 46g, carbohydrate
42g, fat 40g, saturated fat 21g, fibre 3g, added sugar
none, salt 1.2g

Use turkey mince for a change and add
pesto for a taste of the Mediterranean.

Mediterranean Shepherd's Pie

2 onions
2 carrots
1 celery stick
500g pack mince, such as turkey
100g/4oz smoked bacon, chopped
2 tsp plain flour
284ml carton vegetable or
other stock
150ml/¼ pint red wine
700g/1lb 9oz potatoes, peeled
knob of butter
4 tbsp red pesto
25g/1oz parmesan, grated

Takes 1¼ hours • Serves 4

1 Preheat the oven to 200°C/Gas 6/fan oven 180°C from cold. Chop the onions, carrots and celery in a food processor. In a pan over a low heat, cook the mince until the juices start to run, stirring. Add the vegetables and bacon and cook for 15 minutes until browned. Sprinkle over the flour and cook for 1 minute, still stirring. Stir in the stock and wine and cook, covered, for 30 minutes, stirring occasionally.
2 Meanwhile, cut the potatoes into chunks and boil for 10 minutes. Drain well, and return to the pan. Stir in the butter. Season.
3 Stir the pesto into the meat, season and spoon into a shallow ovenproof dish. Spoon the potato pieces on top, sprinkle over the cheese and bake for 30 minutes until golden. Serve immediately.

• Per serving 518 kcalories, protein 42g, carbohydrate 40g, fat 19g, saturated fat 6g, fibre 4g, added sugar none, salt 2.25g

Cooking the onions slowly caramelises them,
adding sweetness.

Chicken with Sweet Onions

1 tbsp olive oil
25g/1oz butter
3 onions, thinly sliced
2 garlic cloves, finely chopped
2 tbsp plain flour
8 skinless chicken thighs
300ml/½ pint unsweetened
apple juice
1 tbsp tomato purée
mashed potatoes or rice, to serve

Takes 1 hour • Serves 4

1 Heat the oil and butter in a large frying pan. Add the onions and stir well. Reduce the heat and cook gently for about 15 minutes until they are softened and dark golden. Add the garlic for the last 5 minutes of cooking time.

2 Transfer the onions and garlic to a plate. Season the flour. Dust the chicken with the flour, shaking off any excess. Cook in the pan for 10 minutes, turning halfway through.

3 Pour in the apple juice and add the tomato purée. Stir well, scraping the bottom of the pan. Return the onions to the pan, cover with a lid and cook for 20–25 minutes, until the chicken is cooked through and the sauce has thickened. Serve with mashed potatoes or rice.

• Per serving 369 kcalories, protein 40g, carbohydrate 24g, fat 13g, saturated fat 6g, fibre 2g, added sugar none, salt 0.57g

Invite everyone to assemble their own tortillas at the table.

Chilli Bean Tortillas

500g pack lamb or beef mince
1 onion, chopped
1 tsp mild chilli powder
1 tsp ground cumin
400g can chopped tomatoes
200g can red kidney beans
8 flour tortillas
handful of shredded
iceberg lettuce leaves
grated cheddar, soured cream and
lemon wedges, to serve

Takes 1 hour 10 minutes • Serves 4

1 Gently heat the mince in a frying pan to release some of the fat. Increase the heat, add the onion and cook for 7 minutes, stirring occasionally to break up the mince. Add the chilli and cumin and cook for 1 minute, stirring. Tip in the tomatoes and kidney beans and bring to the boil.
2 Reduce the heat, cover and cook for 30 minutes until the mince is tender, and then season. Warm the tortillas in the microwave on High for 45 seconds or wrap in foil and put in a preheated oven at 190°C/Gas 5/fan oven 170°C for 5 minutes.
3 Top each tortilla with lettuce and spoon over some chilli mince. Sprinkle with cheese and finish with a little soured cream and a squeeze of lemon juice, then fold the edges over to enclose the filling. Eat immediately.

• Per serving 719 kcalories, protein 41g, carbohydrate 69g, fat 33g, saturated fat 18g, fibre 6g, added sugar none, salt 1.84g

Passata is made from chopped sieved tomatoes.
Buy the version with added basil.

Baked Tomato Burgers

1 tbsp olive oil
1 large onion, finely chopped
500g/1lb 2oz lean minced
lamb or beef
3 tbsp chopped fresh basil
500g jar passata with basil
green salad, to serve

Takes 50 minutes • Serves 4

1 Preheat the oven to 200°C/Gas 6/fan oven 180°C. Heat the oil in a frying pan and cook the onion for about 5 minutes, until soft.
2 Tip the mince and 2 tablespoons of the basil into a bowl, then add the softened onion and season well. Mix together until the ingredients are evenly combined. Shape the mixture into 8–10 flat burgers.
3 Pour about a quarter of the passata into a shallow baking dish. Top with the burgers in a single layer. Heat the remaining passata and basil in the frying pan. Season. Bring to the boil, then pour over the burgers. Bake uncovered for 30 minutes. Serve with a green salad.

• Per serving 297 kcalories, protein 30g, carbohydrate 11g, fat 15g, saturated fat 6g, fibre 1g, added sugar 2g, salt 0.93g

There's a tendency to undercook new potatoes –
be sure they're tender before draining.

New Potato and Mince Curry

450g/1lb lean minced beef or lamb
1 tbsp vegetable oil
1 small onion, chopped
3 garlic cloves, finely chopped
1 tbsp coarsely grated fresh
root ginger
1 fresh red chilli, seeded,
finely sliced
2 tsp ground cumin
2 tsp ground coriander
1 tbsp korma curry paste
500g/1lb 2oz new potatoes
in skins, halved
100g/4oz fresh spinach leaves,
thick stems removed,
leaves torn if large
150ml carton Greek yogurt
chapatis or naan bread, to serve

Takes 1 hour • Serves 4

1 Heat a frying pan and add the mince.
Brown it all over, stirring to break it up.
Remove from the pan and set aside.
Add the oil and onion to the pan and cook
on a medium heat for 5 minutes.
2 Stir in the garlic, spices and curry paste.
Stir fry for 1 minute. Add the mince, potatoes
and 600ml/1 pint water. Bring to the boil,
cover, then simmer for 30 minutes. Season
with salt to taste.
3 Stir in the spinach and simmer for
1 minute, uncovered, until wilted. Swirl in
the yogurt and serve with Indian bread.

• Per serving 353 kcalories, protein 32g, carbohydrate
26g, fat 14g, saturated fat 5g, fibre 2g, added sugar
none, salt 0.54g

For a spicier taste, replace the bacon with 100g/4oz
sliced chorizo or other spicy sausage.

Florentine Potato Gratin

900g/2lb potatoes, any kind
6 rashers back bacon,
smoked or unsmoked
350g/12oz frozen leaf spinach,
preferably freeflow
200ml carton crème fraîche
140g/5oz gruyère or cheddar,
coarsely grated

Takes 40 minutes • Serves 4

1 Preheat the oven to 200°C/Gas 6/fan oven 180°C. Thickly slice the potatoes, then cook in salted boiling water for 7–10 minutes or until just tender. Drain. Meanwhile, grill the bacon until crisp and snip it into large pieces. If using block spinach, defrost it in the microwave, otherwise heat gently in a pan. Freeflow spinach can be used straight from frozen.
2 Layer half the potato slices in a buttered shallow ovenproof dish (about 1.2 litres/ 2 pints). Season lightly, then spread the spinach on top and sprinkle over the bacon. Top with the remaining potato slices. Season.
3 Dot with tablespoonfuls of crème fraîche, then sprinkle with the cheese. Bake for 25 minutes until golden and bubbling. Serve hot from the dish.

• Per serving 617 kcalories, protein 26g, carbohydrate 41g, fat 40g, saturated fat 23g, fibre 5g, added sugar none, salt 2.49g

A colourful gratin that children will love.
Serve with new or jacket potatoes.

Leeks with Ham and Corn

4 leeks, trimmed and halved
widthways, then washed
225g/8oz wafer-thin ham
198g can sweetcorn with
peppers, drained
1 large tomato, seeded
and chopped
25g/1oz butter
25g/1oz plain flour
300ml/½ pint milk
2 tsp wholegrain mustard
50g/2oz cheddar, grated

Takes 50 minutes • Serves 4

1 Preheat the oven to 200°C/Gas 6/fan oven 180°C. Blanch the leeks for 2 minutes. Drain and refresh in cold water, then drain once more really well.

2 Wrap each piece of leek in ham. Arrange them in a buttered 2.25 litre/4 pint rectangular ovenproof dish. Scatter over the sweetcorn and tomato.

3 Put the butter, flour and milk in a pan and bring to the boil, whisking continuously until thickened. Stir in the mustard, simmer for 2–3 minutes, then pour over the leeks. Sprinkle with cheese and bake for 30 minutes until golden. Serve immediately.

• Per serving 303 kcalories, protein 20g, carbohydrate 24g, fat 15g, saturated fat 8g, fibre 4g, added sugar 3g, salt 2.17g

Great for lunch boxes or picnics.
Vegetarians can replace the bacon with mushrooms.

Egg and Bacon Tart

shortcrust pastry made with
175g/6oz plain flour and 85g/3oz
butter bound with 2 tbsp water
5 eggs
4 rashers streaky bacon, chopped
1 large leek, chopped
25g/1oz butter
25g/1oz plain flour
300ml/½ pint milk
2 tsp ready-made mustard
50g/2oz cheddar, grated

Takes 1¼ hours • Serves 4
(with leftovers)

1 Preheat the oven to 200°C/Gas 6/fan oven 180°C from cold. On a floured work surface, roll out the pastry to a 28cm/11in circle. Use to line a 23cm/9in flan tin and trim off the excess. Chill the case for 15 minutes, then bake blind for 15 minutes.
2 Meanwhile, hard-boil two eggs for 8 minutes. Cool, then peel and chop. Dry fry the bacon and leek for 3 minutes until the bacon is crisp. Put the butter, flour and milk in a small pan. Bring slowly to the boil, whisking until thickened. Simmer for 2 minutes. Stir in the mustard.
3 Scatter the leek, bacon and chopped egg over the pastry. Beat the remaining eggs into the sauce and season. Pour into the case, add the cheese and bake for 40 minutes until puffed and golden.

• Per serving 635 kcalories, protein 22g, carbohydrate 44g, fat 42g, saturated fat 23g, fibre 3g, added sugar none, salt 1.9g

Using ready-made pastry saves
preparation time.

Pea and Ham Tart

250g/9oz ready-made
shortcrust pastry
250g/9oz frozen peas, thawed
4 eggs
200ml carton crème fraîche
85g/3oz mature cheddar, grated
85g/3oz slice of thick ham,
cut into chunks

Takes 55 minutes • Serves 6

1 Preheat the oven to 200°C/Gas 6/fan
oven 180°C from cold. Roll out the pastry
and use to line a deep 20–22cm/8–8½in
flan tin. Lightly prick the base with a fork,
fill with crumpled foil and bake blind for
15 minutes.
2 Meanwhile, whizz the peas, eggs, crème
fraîche and seasoning in a food processor
until just blended. Stir in the cheese and ham.
3 Remove the foil from the pastry and lower
the oven temperature to 180°C/Gas 4/fan
oven 160°C. Pour the filling into the pastry
case. Bake for 35 minutes until the filling is
golden and just set. Cool slightly before
removing from the tin. Serve warm or cold.

• Per serving 437 kcalories, protein 16g, carbohydrate
24g, fat 31g, saturated fat 16g, fibre 3g, added sugar
none, salt 1.05g

Leftovers – if you have any –
make great packed lunches.

Ham and Pepper Tart

250g/9oz bought shortcrust pastry
1 onion, finely chopped
1 garlic clove, crushed
1 red pepper, seeded and chopped
1 tbsp olive oil
230g can chopped
tomatoes, drained
100g/4oz wafer-thin ham
handful of black olives (optional)
3 eggs
3 tbsp milk
salad, to serve

Takes 1 hour 10 minutes • Serves 4

1 Preheat the oven to 200°C/Gas 6/fan oven 180°C. Use the pastry to line a 23cm/9in loose-bottomed flan tin. Bake blind for 15 minutes. Remove the paper and beans and cook for 5 minutes.
2 Fry the onion, garlic and red pepper in the oil for 4 minutes until softened. Cool slightly. Lower the oven temperature to 190°C/Gas 5/fan oven 170°C. Tip the onion mixture and tomatoes into the pastry case. Crumple the ham between the vegetables. If using olives, scatter on top.
3 Beat the eggs and milk together, and season. Pour into the case. Bake for 25–30 minutes until set. Serve hot or cold with a salad.

• Per serving 437 kcalories, protein 16g, carbohydrate 35g, fat 27g, saturated fat 10g, fibre 3g, added sugar none, salt 1.22g

A hearty dish that will appeal to the whole family.
You could use other beans instead.

Sausage and Bean Bake

2 tbsp olive oil
12 quality plump herby sausages
1 large onion, cut into wedges
6 rindless streaky bacon
rashers, chopped
4 celery sticks, sliced
2 garlic cloves, crushed
600ml/1 pint vegetable or
chicken stock
3 tbsp tomato purée
400g can cannellini beans, drained
2 tbsp wholegrain mustard
garlic bread, to serve

Takes 40 minutes • Serves 6

1 Preheat the oven to 200°C/Gas 6/fan oven 180°C. Heat half the oil in a frying pan, then brown the sausages all over. Transfer to a roasting tin.
2 Add the remaining oil, the onion, bacon, celery and garlic to the frying pan, and fry until golden. Add the stock and tomato purée. Add the beans, scraping up any bits from the bottom of the pan. Let the stock bubble up, then pour into the roasting tin.
3 Bake, uncovered, for 15–20 minutes. Remove the tin from the oven and stir in the wholegrain mustard, then season. Serve with hot garlic bread.

• Per serving 429 kcalories, protein 23g, carbohydrate 18.2g, fat 30g, saturated fat 9.9g, fibre 3.5g, added sugar none, salt 3.41g

Soak wooden skewers in water for
30 minutes before using to stop them burning.

Pork, Apricot and Ginger Skewers

1 tsp oil
1 small onion, chopped
1 garlic clove, finely chopped
500g pack pork or lamb mince
5cm/2in piece fresh ginger, grated
10 ready-to-eat dried apricots,
finely chopped
handful of chopped fresh parsley
300g/10oz long grain rice
½ tsp turmeric
juice of ½ lemon
142ml carton natural yogurt
rice, to serve

Takes 55 minutes • Serves 4

1 Preheat the oven to 200°C/Gas 6/fan oven 180°C, or the grill to high. Heat the oil in a pan, then fry the onion and garlic for 5 minutes. Cool slightly, then tip into a bowl with the mince, ginger, apricots and half the parsley. Season.
2 Divide the mixture into four and mould around the skewers. If cooking in the oven transfer to a roasting tin and cook for 20 minutes, otherwise put the tin under the hot grill, turning occasionally, for 10 minutes until browned.
3 Boil the rice with 600ml/1 pint water and the turmeric, covered, for about 12–15 minutes until tender and the water has been absorbed. Stir the rest of the parsley and the lemon into the yogurt and drizzle over the skewers. Serve with rice.

• Per serving 536 kcalories, protein 32g, carbohydrate 75g, fat 14g, saturated fat 5g, fibre 1g, added sugar none, salt 0.31g

Prepare the meatloaf, minus the topping,
the night before. Press into the tin, cover and chill.

Pork and Herb Meatloaf

1 tbsp oil
1 onion, finely chopped
2 smoked streaky bacon rashers,
rinded and chopped
500g pack pork mince
100g/4oz fresh breadcrumbs
1 medium egg, beaten
1 tsp salt
2 tbsp tomato purée
1 tbsp dried tarragon or thyme
salad and new potatoes, to serve

FOR THE TOPPING
2 smoked streaky bacon rashers
25g/1oz breadcrumbs
50g/2oz cheddar, grated

Takes 1 hour 25 minutes • Serves 4

1 Preheat the oven to 180°C/Gas 4/fan oven 160°C. Heat the oil in a frying pan and fry the onion for 3–4 minutes until softened. Transfer to a bowl. Mix in the bacon, pork, breadcrumbs, egg, salt, tomato purée and dried herbs. Press into a 450g/1lb loaf tin. Bake, uncovered, for 1 hour.
2 To make the topping, dry fry the bacon until crisp. Remove from the pan. Fry the breadcrumbs in the bacon fat for 2 minutes until just golden. Stir into a bowl with the cheese and crumble in the bacon.
3 Five minutes before the end of cooking, sprinkle the topping over the meatloaf. Return to the oven for 5 minutes to melt the cheese. Leave to stand for 10 minutes. Loosen the sides with a knife and remove. Slice and serve with a salad and new potatoes.

• Per serving 488 kcalories, protein 37g, carbohydrate 29g, fat 26g, saturated fat 10g, fibre 1g, added sugar none, salt 3.01g

Pimientos are peppers that have been roasted,
peeled and seeded, then packed into cans.

Lemon and Thyme Meatballs

2 slices white bread, crusts removed
and torn in pieces
2 tbsp milk
500g pack pork mince
finely grated zest of 1 lemon
2 tsp dried thyme
1 garlic clove, finely chopped
1 tbsp olive oil
1 small onion, finely chopped
250g/9oz chestnut
mushrooms, sliced
285g can pimientos,
drained and chopped
200ml carton crème fraîche
350g/12oz rigatoni, cooked and
drained, to serve

Takes 1 hour 10 minutes • Serves 4

1 Soak the bread in the milk for 5 minutes.
Squeeze out the excess milk, then put the
bread in a bowl with the mince, lemon zest,
thyme and garlic. Season. Mix well and
shape into 20 balls.
2 Heat the oil in a frying pan. Cover and
cook the meatballs for 20 minutes, turning,
until they are evenly browned. Remove and
keep warm.
3 Add the onion to the pan and cook for
5 minutes until softened but not brown. Add
the mushrooms and cook for 8 minutes until
beginning to brown. Stir in the pimientos and
crème fraîche, heat through and season. Stir
the pasta into the sauce, spoon on to plates
and top with the meatballs.

• Per serving 753 kcalories, protein 38g, carbohydrate
73g, fat 36g, saturated fat 14g, fibre 4g, added sugar
none, salt 0.67g

A simple topping makes ordinary pork
chops fit for a feast.

Pork Chops with Gorgonzola

4 large boneless pork loin chops,
140–225g/5–8oz each
1 tbsp olive oil
1 tbsp green pesto
3 small tomatoes, thinly sliced
100g/4oz gorgonzola, cut into
4 thick slices
new potatoes and salad, to serve

Takes 20 minutes • Serves 4

1 Preheat the grill to high. Brush the chops with the olive oil and season well. Lay the chops on a baking sheet and grill for 4–5 minutes. Turn over and cook for a further 4–5 minutes.

2 Remove the chops from the grill. Brush each one with the pesto. Put the tomato slices on top of the chops and add the slices of cheese.

3 Put the chops back under the grill for 2–4 minutes, until the cheese is bubbling and has melted. Serve immediately with new potatoes and a salad.

• Per serving 351 kcalories, protein 36g, carbohydrate 1g, fat 22g, saturated fat 9g, fibre none, added sugar none, salt 1.11g

This tasty relish keeps well in the fridge.
Serve it with sausages or burgers too.

Roast Pork with Onion Marmalade

2 x 300–350g/10–12oz pork fillets
boiled potatoes, to serve

FOR THE MARMALADE
450g/1lb onions, peeled and
thinly sliced
25g/1oz butter
85g/3oz light muscovado sugar
100ml/3½fl oz red wine vinegar

Takes 1 hour 5 minutes • Serves 4

1 Preheat the oven to 190°C/Gas 5/fan oven 170°C from cold. Put the pork fillets in a roasting tin and season. Roast for 25–30 minutes until cooked through.
2 Meanwhile, cook the onions in a pan with the butter for 10 minutes, until softened and lightly browned. Stir in the sugar and red wine vinegar and cook uncovered for a further 25–30 minutes, stirring occasionally, until the onions are slightly caramelised and very soft.
3 Remove the pork from the oven. Cover with foil and leave for 5 minutes before slicing into thick pieces. Spoon over the warm onion marmalade and serve with boiled potatoes.

• Per serving 346 kcalories, protein 34g, carbohydrate 29g, fat 11g, saturated fat 5g, fibre 2g, added sugar 20g, salt 0.63g

Rösti are small cakes of grated potato. Here, tuna is added
to make a meal of one frying-pan-sized rösti.

Tuna Rösti

750g/1lb 10oz potatoes, unpeeled
3 tbsp sunflower oil
1 large onion, sliced
200g can tuna, drained
4 eggs
2 × 400g cans baked beans

Takes 45 minutes • Serves 4

1 Cook the potatoes, in their skins, in salted
boiling water for 10 minutes. Meanwhile,
heat a tablespoon of the oil in a frying pan
and fry the onion until golden. Drain the
potatoes and, when cool enough to handle,
peel. Grate them coarsely into a bowl. Add
the onion, tuna and seasoning and mix well.
2 Heat the remaining oil in the frying pan.
Press the potato mixture into it with a spatula
to make a large cake. Cook very gently for
10 minutes until the underside is golden.
Put a large plate on top of the pan and turn
the rösti out onto it. Slide it back into the pan
and cook the other side for 8–10 minutes.
3 Meanwhile, fry the eggs and heat up the
beans in a pan. Slide the rösti out of the pan
onto a serving plate. Cut into wedges and
serve with the fried eggs and baked beans.

• Per serving 511 kcalories, protein 30g, carbohydrate
67g, fat 16g, saturated fat 3g, fibre 10g, added sugar
7g, salt 3.34g

Puff pastry rectangles,
cooked separately, become the pie 'lids'.

Easy Tuna Puff Pie

375g packet rolled ready-to-use
puff pastry
25g/1oz butter
1 onion, chopped
1 small red pepper,
seeded and chopped
25g/1oz plain flour
600ml/1 pint milk
700g/1lb 9oz potato, peeled and
cut into big chunks
225g/8oz broccoli, cut into florets
185g can tuna chunks
in brine, drained
handful of chopped fresh parsley

Takes 45 minutes • Serves 4

1 Preheat the oven to 200°C/Gas 6/fan
oven 180°C. Cut out four 13 × 10cm/
5 × 4in pastry rectangles. Place on a baking
sheet, lightly slash the tops diagonally and
bake for 15–18 minutes, until they are
golden and puffed.
2 Meanwhile, melt the butter in a pan, then
fry the onion and pepper until soft but not
brown. Add the flour and cook, stirring,
for 1 minute. Stir in the milk gradually.
Cook, stirring, until thickened slightly.
3 Add the potatoes and simmer,
covered, for 10 minutes. Add the broccoli
and simmer for 10 minutes until tender. Stir
the tuna into the sauce and heat through.
Season, add the parsley and spoon on to
serving plates. Top each serving with a
pastry lid.

• Per serving 721 kcalories, protein 26g, carbohydrate
82g, fat 34g, saturated fat 7g, fibre 5g, added sugar
none, salt 1.42g

A tub of pesto makes an instant, tasty dressing.
The spinach softens in the heat of the potatoes.

Warm Potato and Tuna Salad

650g/1lb 7oz new potatoes,
halved lengthways if large
2 tbsp pesto (fresh is best)
4 tbsp olive oil
8 cherry tomatoes
175g can tuna, drained
225g/8oz green beans, halved
couple of handfuls of spinach
(preferably baby leaves),
tear if larger
crusty bread, to serve

Takes 20 minutes • Serves 4

1 Put the potatoes in a pan of salted boiling water, bring back to the boil and simmer for 8–10 minutes.
2 Meanwhile, mix together the pesto and oil. Halve the tomatoes, and drain and flake the tuna. Add the beans to the potatoes for the last 3 minutes of cooking time.
3 Drain the potatoes and beans and tip into a salad bowl. Stir in the spinach so it wilts a little in the warmth from the vegetables. Season. Scatter over the tomatoes and tuna, drizzle over the pesto and toss together. Serve with crusty bread.

• Per serving 336 kcalories, protein 15g, carbohydrate 28g, fat 19g, saturated fat 3g, fibre 3g, added sugar none, salt 0.45g

Instead of using soup, you could use mushroom or tomato pasta sauce from the chiller cabinet.

Tuna and Broccoli Pasta Bake

300g/10oz penne or rigatoni
400g/14oz broccoli,
cut into small florets
200g can tuna, drained
295g can condensed
mushroom soup
150ml/¼ pint milk
100g/4oz cheddar, grated
1 small packet salted crisps

Takes 30 minutes • Serves 4

1 Preheat the oven to 200°C/Gas 6/fan oven 180°C. Cook the pasta in salted boiling water for 10–12 minutes. Add the broccoli for the last 3 minutes of cooking, then drain.
2 Tip the pasta and broccoli into a shallow ovenproof dish. Scatter the tuna over. Mix the soup with the milk, then pour over the pasta and toss it all together gently.
3 Scatter over two-thirds of the cheese. Lightly crush the crisps in the bag, then sprinkle over the pasta. Top with the remaining cheese. Bake for 15 minutes until the topping is golden. Serve immediately.

• Per serving 572 kcalories, protein 33g, carbohydrate 69g, fat 20g, saturated fat 8g, fibre 5g, added sugar none, salt 2.41g

A simple and filling supper made
from a can of salmon.

Potato and Salmon Grill

650g/1lb 7oz new potatoes, skin on,
sliced lengthways
100g/4oz frozen peas
200g can salmon
200ml carton crème fraîche
100g/4oz mature cheddar,
coarsely grated

Takes 25 minutes • Serves 4

1 Boil the potatoes in salted water for
about 10 minutes, until almost tender but
not breaking up. Tip in the frozen peas and
simmer for another 2–3 minutes. Drain well
then tip into a mixing bowl. Preheat the grill
to high.

2 Drain the salmon and flake into chunks,
then gently toss with the potatoes and peas.
Season to taste and spoon into a shallow
flameproof dish.

3 Dollop the crème fraîche on top, roughly
spread it over, and then scatter over the
cheese. Grill for a few minutes until bubbling
and golden.

• Per serving 465 kcalories, protein 22g, carbohydrate
31g, fat 29g, saturated fat 15g, fibre 3g, added sugar
none, salt 1.10g

Think you don't have time to make a casserole?
You do in a microwave.

Salmon and Sweetcorn Casserole

2 leeks, about 300g/10oz in total
700g/1lb 9oz floury potatoes,
such as King Edward
300ml/½ pint full-fat milk
300ml/½ pint vegetable stock
200g can sweetcorn with
peppers, drained
450g/1lb skinless salmon fillet
cut into 2.5cm/1in cubes
good splash of Tabasco
handful of chopped fresh parsley

Takes 25 minutes • Serves 4

1 Halve the leeks lengthways, then slice. Set aside. Peel the potatoes, cut into cubes and put in a microwave-proof bowl with the milk and stock.
2 Cook the potatoes on High for 8 minutes until they're starting to soften. Add the leeks and cook for 5 minutes. Stir well with a fork, pressing about half the potato cubes against the side of the bowl to break up and thicken the stock.
3 Stir in the sweetcorn and salmon, and season. Cook on High for 3 minutes until the salmon is just cooked through. Stir in the Tabasco and parsley. Serve immediately.

• Per serving 453 kcalories, protein 32g, carbohydrate 47g, fat 17g, saturated fat 4g, fibre 5g, added sugar 3g, salt 0.85g

Salmon fillets are always on special offer somewhere, but still seem luxurious.

Orange Crumb Salmon

85g/3oz fresh breadcrumbs
(2 thick slices white bread)
2 tbsp olive oil, plus extra
for greasing
finely grated zest and
juice of 1 orange
4 tbsp chopped fresh parsley
4 boneless skinless salmon fillets,
about 140g/5oz each in weight
700g/1lb 9oz new potatoes
3 tbsp mayonnaise

Takes 35 minutes • Serves 4

1 Preheat the oven to 200°C/Gas 6/fan oven 180°C. Mix together the breadcrumbs, oil, orange zest and half the parsley. Season.
2 Put the salmon fillets on a baking sheet lined with lightly greased foil. Press the orange crumbs on to each fillet so they stick. Bake for 15–20 minutes until the salmon is just cooked and the topping is golden.
3 Meanwhile, cook the potatoes in a pan of salted boiling water for 12–15 minutes until tender, then drain. Stir the remaining parsley into the mayonnaise and thin with a little bit of the orange juice, until it has the consistency of single cream. Serve the salmon with the new potatoes and the herb mayonnaise.

• Per serving 611 kcalories, protein 34g, carbohydrate 46g, fat 33g, saturated fat 6g, fibre 3g, added sugar none, salt 0.8g

You could use well-drained canned
salmon in place of fresh fish.

Salmon and Dill Fishcakes

700g/1lb 9oz potatoes,
cut into chunks
100ml/3½fl oz milk
300g/10oz boneless skinless
salmon fillet
knob of butter
1 small onion, finely chopped
2 tsp creamed horseradish sauce
1 heaped tbsp chopped fresh dill
vegetable oil, for frying
1 egg, beaten
225g/8oz dry breadcrumbs
chips or new potatoes, and tomato
and onion salad, to serve

Takes 40 minutes • Serves 4

1 Cook the potatoes in salted boiling water
for 15 minutes until tender. Drain and mash.
Put the milk and salmon in a frying pan.
Bring to the boil, cover with foil and simmer
for 3–4 minutes until just cooked. Take off
the heat and stand for 5 minutes. Drain and
flake the fish. Reserve the milk.
2 Heat the butter in a pan and cook the
onion for 3–4 minutes. Mix into the mash
with two tablespoons of the reserved milk,
the horseradish and dill. Season. Stir in the
flaked fish.
3 Shape the mixture into eight cakes. Heat
1cm/½in oil in a frying pan. Dip each cake in
egg, then breadcrumbs. Fry for 5 minutes,
turning halfway, until golden. Serve with
chips or new potatoes and a salad.

• Per serving 644 kcalories, protein 27g, carbohydrate
72g, fat 92g, saturated fat 6g, fibre 4g, added sugar
none, salt 1.27g

Crushed crackers make an especially
crispy coating for fishcakes.

Crisp Cod and Corn Cakes

4 tbsp milk
500g/1lb 2oz cod fillet
198g can sweetcorn, drained
6 spring onions, finely chopped
750g/1lb 10oz floury potatoes,
cooked and mashed with butter
2 eggs
12 cream crackers, crushed into
fine crumbs
oil, for shallow frying
salad leaves and tomato sauce,
to serve

Takes 35 minutes • Serves 4

1 Put the milk and fish in a frying pan. Bring to the boil, cover and cook for 4–5 minutes, depending on the thickness of the fish. It should flake easily. Set aside until cool enough to handle.
2 Stir the corn and onions into the mash and season. Remove the fish with a slotted spoon and stir into the mash, taking care not to break it up too much. Divide into eight and shape into round cakes.
3 Beat the eggs lightly with a fork. Dip the cakes in the egg, then in the cracker crumbs. Heat a little oil in a frying pan and cook the cakes, four at a time, for about 3 minutes. Carefully turn and cook for 2–3 minutes until crisp and golden. Serve with a salad and some tomato sauce.

• Per serving 628 kcalories, protein 33g, carbohydrate 57g, fat 31g, saturated fat 8g, fibre 3g, added sugar 3g, salt 1.3g

Eat mackerel when it is as fresh as possible and
still glossy, for the best flavour.

Mackerel Baked in Foil

2 whole mackerel
1 lemon
4 fresh rosemary sprigs
2 garlic cloves, sliced
1 small red onion, thinly sliced
4 tbsp cider or apple juice
boiled potatoes, sprinkled with
parsley, to serve

Takes 30 minutes • Serves 2

1 Preheat the oven to 200°C/Gas 6/fan
oven 180°C from cold. Put each fish on a
large square of foil or baking paper on a
baking sheet. Season the fish inside and out.
2 Slice the lemon, then cut each slice in
half. Tuck lemon slices inside each fish with
a couple of rosemary sprigs and a few garlic
slices. Scatter over the onion and pour two
tablespoons of cider or apple juice over
each fish.
3 Wrap the foil or baking paper loosely
around each fish to make a parcel and bake
for 25 minutes. Serve with boiled potatoes
sprinkled with parsley.

• Per serving 460 kcalories, protein 37g, carbohydrate
7g, fat 31g, saturated fat 6g, fibre 1g, added sugar
none, salt 0.32g

An easy supper for a crowd,
this dish is cooked and served in one tin.

Prawn and Tomato Pasta Bake

450g/1lb leeks, thinly sliced
900g/2lb ripe tomatoes, quartered
3 tbsp olive oil
600g/1lb 5oz pasta shapes,
such as penne or rigatoni
225g/8oz peeled prawns,
thawed if frozen
2 tbsp sun-dried tomato paste
150ml/¼ pint vegetable stock
3 tbsp roughly chopped
fresh parsley
142ml carton double cream
150g ball mozzarella,
grated or finely chopped
4 tbsp freshly grated parmesan
1 thick slice of bread,
made into crumbs

Takes 1¼ hours • Serves 8

1 Preheat the oven to 200°C/Gas 6/fan oven 180°C from cold. Put the leeks and tomatoes in a large roasting tin and drizzle over the olive oil. Season and mix well. Roast for 30 minutes.
2 Meanwhile, cook the pasta for about 10–12 minutes until tender and then drain. Tip into the roasting tin along with the prawns. Season. Mix the tomato paste into the stock and stir into the pasta. Sprinkle over the parsley, then drizzle with cream. Sprinkle over the mozzarella, parmesan and the breadcrumbs.
3 Return to the oven for 15–20 minutes until the topping is crisp and golden. Serve straight from the tin.

• Per serving 506 kcalories, protein 21g, carbohydrate 65g, fat 20g, saturated fat 9g, fibre 5g, added sugar none, salt 0.65g

Skinless chicken breasts get a colourful
coating and a flavour boost.

Chicken with a Red Pepper Crust

4 boneless skinless chicken breasts
1 small red pepper, seeded
2 garlic cloves
large handful of fresh parsley
2 tbsp olive oil
pasta or new potatoes, and
green salad, to serve

Takes 30 minutes • Serves 4

1 Preheat the oven to 200°C/Gas 6/fan
oven 180°C. Put the chicken breasts in
a roasting tin or shallow ovenproof dish.
Season.
2 Roughly chop the red pepper and finely
chop the garlic. Put in a food processor
with the parsley and pulse a few times until
coarsely chopped. Stir in the oil and season
generously. Spread the crust over the chicken.
3 Spoon two tablespoons of water into
the base of the dish and roast the chicken,
uncovered, for 25 minutes. Serve with pasta
or new potatoes and a green salad.

• Per serving 210 kcalories, protein 23g, carbohydrate
5g, fat 11g, saturated fat 2g, fibre 1g, added sugar
none, salt 0.19g

Couscous is the perfect partner for this dish and will only need soaking then fluffing up with a fork.

Moroccan Chicken

4 boneless skinless chicken thighs,
500g/1lb 2oz in total
300ml/½ pint chicken or
vegetable stock
2 onions, finely chopped
3 tbsp olive oil
1 tbsp clear honey
1 tsp each ground cumin
and coriander
good pinch each of chilli powder
and ground cinnamon
225g/8oz courgettes, cut into sticks
400g can chickpeas, drained
3 tbsp chopped fresh parsley
juice of 1 lemon
couscous or cooked rice, to serve

Takes 50 minutes • Serves 4

1 Put the chicken, stock, onions, oil, honey, herbs and spices in a pan, and season. Bring to the boil, cover and cook gently for 25 minutes until the chicken is tender.
2 Add the courgettes and chickpeas and cook for 10 minutes.
3 Stir in the parsley and the lemon juice. Season to taste. Serve with couscous or rice.

• Per serving 539 kcalories, protein 39g, carbohydrate 52g, fat 21g, saturated fat 4g, fibre 6g, added sugar 3g, salt 1.12g

Cooked this way, the chicken develops
a delicious sweet-sour, sticky coating.

Lemon and Honey Chicken

3 lemons
50g/2oz butter
3 tbsp clear honey
1 garlic clove, finely chopped
4 rosemary sprigs, leaves stripped
from the stalks
8 chicken pieces, such as
thighs and drumsticks
750g/1lb 10oz potatoes,
cut into smallish chunks
green salad, to serve

Takes 1 hour 20 minutes • Serves 4

1 Preheat the oven to 200°C/Gas 6/fan oven 180°C from cold. Squeeze the juice from two lemons and put in a small pan with the butter, honey, garlic and rosemary, and season. Heat gently until the butter melts.
2 Arrange the chicken in one layer in a shallow roasting tin. Put the potatoes around the chicken. Drizzle the lemon butter over the chicken and potatoes, turning the potatoes until evenly coated. Cut the remaining lemon into eight wedges and nestle them among the potatoes.
3 Roast the chicken for 50 minutes to 1 hour, stirring a couple of times, until the chicken is cooked and the potatoes are crisp and golden. Serve with a green salad.

• Per serving 647 kcalories, protein 39g, carbohydrate 47g, fat 35g, saturated fat 14g, fibre 3g, added sugar 12g, salt 0.06g

Vary the vegetables – add fine green beans or
mangetout instead of asparagus and sugar snap peas.

Chicken with Spring Vegetables

2 tbsp olive oil
1 onion, finely chopped
4 boneless skinless chicken thighs,
each cut in half
700g/1lb 9oz new potatoes,
halved if large
225g/8oz carrots, sliced
1 bay leaf
300ml/½ pint chicken stock
200g pack sugar snap peas
250g/9oz asparagus, sliced
juice of 1 lemon
handful of fresh tarragon, chopped
200ml carton crème fraîche

Takes 40 minutes • Serves 4

1 Heat the oil in a large pan, add the onion
and chicken and cook for 5 minutes until the
chicken starts to brown. Add the potatoes,
carrots and bay leaf and fry for 3 minutes,
stirring to prevent the chicken from sticking.
Pour in the stock and then season.
2 Bring to the boil, then cover and simmer
for 20 minutes, until the potatoes and
chicken are cooked. Add the sugar snap
peas and asparagus and cook for a further
3 minutes.
3 Remove the bay leaf and stir in the lemon
juice, tarragon and crème fraîche. Check the
seasoning and serve.

• Per serving 511 kcalories, protein 32g, carbohydrate
41g, fat 25g, saturated fat 10g, fibre 5g, added sugar
none, salt 0.71g

A substantial meal in one –
no accompaniments needed.

Chicken and Red Pepper Pie

2 tbsp vegetable oil
1 small onion, chopped
3 boneless skinless chicken breasts,
cut into chunks
1 red pepper, seeded and sliced
175g/6oz broccoli, cut into small
florets (including stems), chopped
425g pack ready-rolled puff pastry
(with 2 sheets), thawed
150g carton fresh ready-made
cheese and chive dip
milk or beaten egg, to glaze

Takes 1 hour • Serves 4

1 Heat the oil in a frying pan and fry the onion for about 3 minutes, until starting to brown. Add the chicken and cook, stirring, for 5 minutes. Tip in the pepper and broccoli and fry for 8–10 minutes, until everything is just cooked. Season. Cool slightly. Preheat the oven to 200°C/Gas 6/fan oven 180°C.
2 Put a rolled pastry sheet on a dampened baking sheet. Spoon over the chicken mixture, leaving a 2.5cm/1in border all the way round. Dot spoonfuls of dip all over. Brush the pastry edges with water, top with the other pastry sheet and fold the edges of the bottom sheet over the top one, pressing to seal. Make light slashes on the surface.
3 Brush the pastry with milk or beaten egg and bake for 25–30 minutes, until the pastry is puffed and golden.

• Per serving 727 kcalories, protein 35g, carbohydrate 46g, fat 46g, saturated fat 1g, fibre 2g, added sugar none, salt 1.33g

Make a breast of chicken go further
with canned chickpeas and frozen vegetables.

Chicken and Chickpea Chilli

1 tbsp olive oil
1 large onion, roughly chopped
1 boneless skinless chicken
breast, sliced
2 garlic cloves, finely chopped
1 tbsp chilli powder
1 tsp ground cumin
400g can chopped tomatoes
450ml/16fl oz vegetable stock
1 tsp sugar
400g can chickpeas, drained
300g/10oz frozen veg, including
carrots, cauliflower and broccoli

TO SERVE
142ml carton soured cream
50g/2oz grated cheddar
generous handful of tortilla chips

Takes 50 minutes • Serves 4

1 Heat the oil in a large saucepan and fry
the onion for 5–6 minutes until golden. Add
the chicken and fry until golden brown. Add
the garlic and spices and cook for 1 minute.
2 Stir in the tomatoes, stock and sugar.
Bring to the boil, cover and simmer for
25 minutes. Add the chickpeas and the
frozen vegetables, bring back to the boil,
then simmer for 10 minutes.
3 Season to taste. Serve with a spoonful of
soured cream, a sprinkling of cheddar and
some tortilla chips on the side.

• Per serving 374 kcalories, protein 22.8g, carbohydrate
28.3g, fat 19.6g, saturated fat 7.9g, fibre 6.3g, added
sugar 1.3g, salt 1.51g

Frozen oven chips and chops cooked
together in one tin in the oven.

Lamb Chop and Chip Bake

3 tbsp olive oil
2 large onions, peeled and sliced
750g bag frozen hot and spicy
potato wedges
8 small lamb chops
1 tsp dried thyme
150ml/¼ pint lamb or chicken stock
1 tbsp tomato purée

Takes 40 minutes • Serves 4

1 Preheat the oven to 230°C/Gas 8/fan
oven 210°C. Heat a large roasting tin on
the hob, then add two tablespoons of the
olive oil.
2 Put the onions in the tin and fry for
about 5 minutes, stirring often, until golden.
Remove from the heat. Scatter over the
potato wedges. Put the chops on top,
sprinkle over the thyme and drizzle over the
remaining oil.
3 Bake for 20 minutes. Mix the stock
with the tomato purée and pour around the
chops in the tin. Bake for 10 minutes until
everything is brown and crisp. Season and
then serve.

• Per serving 680 kcalories, protein 33g, carbohydrate
39g, fat 45g, saturated fat 19g, fibre 4g, added sugar
none, salt 0.43g

A good supper choice for people
who can't get boiled rice right.

One-pot Lamb with Rice

2 tbsp olive oil
650g/1½ lb boneless lamb
(leg or shoulder), cut into
2.5cm/1in cubes
2 onions, roughly chopped
2 tsp ground cumin
2 tsp ground coriander
175g/6oz long grain rice
2 tsp dried oregano
3 tbsp tomato purée
grated zest and juice of 1 lemon
2 tbsp chopped fresh parsley

Takes 55 minutes • Serves 4

1 Heat the oil in a large frying pan with a lid. Add the lamb and cook over a high heat, stirring constantly, for 5 minutes, until browned on all sides. Add the onions and cook for a further 2–3 minutes until softened. Add the cumin and coriander and fry for a further minute.
2 Stir in the rice and oregano. Mix the purée, lemon zest and juice with 850ml/1½ pints boiling water and pour into the pan. Stir well and season.
3 Bring to the boil, then simmer for 20–25 minutes until the lamb and rice are cooked. Stir in the parsley and serve straight from the pan.

• Per serving 563 kcalories, protein 36g, carbohydrate 47g, fat 27g, saturated fat 11g, fibre 1g, added sugar none, salt 0.34g

Dates and cranberry sauce add sweetness
and succulence to the lamb.

Lamb and Date Casserole

550g/1lb 4oz diced lamb
1 tbsp plain flour
2 tbsp olive oil
2 onions, chopped
3 large carrots, cut into chunks
2 garlic cloves, finely chopped
600ml/1 pint chicken, lamb or
vegetable stock
1 tbsp cranberry sauce
2 tsp tomato purée
12 pitted ready-to-eat dates
3 tbsp chopped fresh parsley
rice or steamed couscous, to serve

Takes 1 hour • Serves 4

1 Put the lamb and flour in a plastic bag and shake well, until coated. Heat the olive oil in a large frying pan. Remove the lamb from the bag and shake off any excess flour, then add to the pan with the onions and carrots. Cook over a medium to high heat for 8–10 minutes, stirring often, until golden.
2 Stir in the garlic and cook for 1 minute. Pour in the stock and bring to the boil. Reduce the heat and simmer, covered, for 20 minutes, until thickened slightly.
3 Stir in the cranberry sauce, tomato purée, dates and parsley. Season to taste. Serve with rice or steamed couscous.

• Per serving 466 kcalories, protein 32g, carbohydrate 48g, fat 18g, saturated fat 6g, fibre 5g, added sugar 1g, salt 0.81g

You can make up the savoury bean mix
a day ahead of cooking the chops.

Lamb and Haricot Hotpot

2 onions, chopped
3 tbsp olive oil
2 garlic cloves, chopped
2 × 400g can haricot beans,
drained (or use cannellini or
flageolet beans instead)
1 tsp dried oregano
150ml/¼ pint vegetable stock
200g can chopped tomatoes
8 lamb chops or 4 lamb leg steaks

Takes 55 minutes • Serves 4

1 Preheat the oven to 200°C/Gas 6/fan oven 180°C from cold. Fry the onions in two tablespoons of the oil for 5 minutes. Add the garlic, beans and half the oregano and stir briefly. Add the stock and tomatoes, season, then bring to the boil.
2 Tip the bean mixture into an ovenproof dish that will accommodate the chops in a single layer. Lay the chops on top.
3 Sprinkle with the remaining oregano, drizzle with the remaining oil and season. Cook in the oven for 30 minutes until the chops are tender and nicely browned.

• Per serving 518 kcalories, protein 39g, carbohydrate 30g, fat 28g, saturated fat 10g, fibre 9g, added sugar none, salt 1.67g

A lighter version of a popular dish, using pork instead
of beef and green beans in place of red kidney beans.

Summer Chilli

2 tbsp oil
1 onion, chopped
500g pork mince
2 garlic cloves, crushed
2 tsp mild chilli powder
400g can chopped tomatoes
2 tbsp tomato purée
600ml/1 pint chicken stock
1 red pepper, seeded and
cut into chunks
350g/12oz new potatoes,
cut into chunks
250g/9oz green beans, trimmed
warm crusty bread, to serve

Takes 50 minutes • Serves 4

1 Heat the oil in a large frying pan, then fry
the onion and pork mince for 3–4 minutes,
stirring occasionally.
2 Add the crushed garlic, chilli powder,
tomatoes, tomato purée, chicken stock,
red pepper and new potatoes. Bring to the
boil, cover and simmer over a low heat for
15 minutes until the potatoes are just tender.
3 Stir in the green beans, re-cover the pan
and continue to cook for 5 minutes, until the
beans are tender but crisp. Serve with warm
crusty bread.

• Per serving 390 kcalories, protein 30g, carbohydrate
26g, fat 19g, saturated fat 5g, fibre 4g, added sugar
none, salt 0.94g

Pork mince is economical when feeding a crowd.
Sliced potatoes make it filling.

Pork and Potato Hotpot

1 tbsp olive oil
1 onion, chopped
2 garlic cloves, crushed
1kg/2lb 4oz minced pork
1 tbsp plain flour
425ml/¾ pint chicken or
vegetable stock
1 tsp dried rosemary or thyme
2 tbsp Worcestershire sauce
4 tbsp tomato purée
1.5kg/3lb 5oz potatoes, peeled
25g/1oz butter
steamed green vegetables, to serve

Takes 2 hours • Serves 8

1 Preheat the oven to 190°C/Gas 5/fan oven 170°C. Heat the oil and fry the onion and garlic for 3–4 minutes. Add the mince and fry for a further 5–6 minutes.
2 Stir in the flour and cook for 1 minute. Add the stock, then stir in the rosemary or thyme, Worcestershire sauce and tomato purée. Bring to the boil, then simmer for 30 minutes. Meanwhile, cook the potatoes in salted boiling water for 10 minutes. Drain and slice thickly.
3 Spoon half the mince mixture into a 20 × 30 × 5–7cm (8 × 12 × 2–3in deep) ovenproof dish and cover with half the potatoes. Repeat the layers, dot the top with the butter and bake for 1 hour. Serve with steamed green vegetables.

• Per serving 407 kcalories, protein 29g, carbohydrate 38g, fat 17g, saturated fat 6g, fibre 3g, added sugar none, salt 0.64g

A really quick and easy meal –
the perfect (lazy!) TV supper.

Sausage and Corn Hash

1 tbsp olive oil
400g/14oz sausages
(use your favourite)
700g/1lb 9oz new potatoes,
cut into chunks
165g can sweetcorn, drained
2 tbsp chopped fresh coriander
or parsley
226g jar spicy tomato salsa,
to serve

Takes 30 minutes • Serves 4

1 Heat the oil in a large frying pan. Cut the sausages into bite-sized chunks and fry in the oil until just cooked, about 10 minutes. Meanwhile, bring a large pan of salted water to the boil, add the potatoes and cook for 8–10 minutes. Drain well.

2 Tip the potatoes into the frying pan, season and fry over a medium heat until they take on a bit of colour. Stir in the sweetcorn and heat through. Season.

3 Sprinkle with coriander or parsley. Divide between serving dishes and drizzle some salsa over the hash.

• Per serving 519 kcalories, protein 17g, carbohydrate 56g, fat 27g, saturated fat 9g, fibre 4g, added sugar 4g, salt 4.09g

A straightforward recipe using
affordable ingredients.

Mustardy Sausages with Apple

1 tbsp vegetable oil
8 plump herby sausages,
about 450g/1lb
1 medium onion, cut into wedges
2 Cox's or other eating apples
(skin left on), cored and
each cut into 8 wedges
1 rounded tbsp redcurrant jelly
300ml/½ pint chicken stock
(made from a cube is fine)
2 tbsp mustard, preferably grainy
a few rosemary twigs

Takes 25 minutes • Serves 4

1 Heat the oil in a large frying pan, add the sausages and fry for 5 minutes, turning often. Nestle in the onion wedges and continue to fry, until everything is starting to go really golden, stirring every now and then. Turn up the heat, toss in the apples and let them take on a bit of colour too, stirring carefully so that they don't break up.
2 Stir the redcurrant jelly into the stock until it dissolves, then stir in the mustard. Pour this into the frying pan so everything bubbles madly for a few minutes to make a syrupy gravy.
3 Lower the heat, throw in the rosemary and simmer, uncovered, for 10 minutes until the sausages are cooked.

• Per serving 368 kcalories, protein 16.7g, carbohydrate 21g, fat 24.7g, saturated fat 8.1g, fibre 2g, added sugar 3.2g, salt 2.68g

Wholegrain mustard adds
a kick to a favourite family supper.

Mustardy Toad

8 plump herby sausages
2 onions, thinly sliced
1 tbsp vegetable oil
100g/4oz plain flour
2 eggs
300ml/½ pint equal mix
of milk and water
2 tbsp wholegrain mustard
cabbage or broccoli,
and gravy to serve

Takes 1 hour • Serves 4

1 Preheat the oven to 220°C/Gas 7/fan oven 200°C. Put the sausages and onions in a roasting tin and drizzle with the oil. Roast for 15–20 minutes until the sausages just start to colour.
2 Sift the flour and a pinch of salt and pepper into a bowl. Make a well in the centre, drop in the eggs and beat together. Gradually beat in half the milk mixture, then stir in the remaining liquid and the mustard.
3 Remove the roasting tin from the oven. Quickly pour over the batter and return to the oven for a further 35–40 minutes, until the batter is risen and golden. Serve with some cabbage or broccoli, and gravy.

• Per serving 562 kcalories, protein 24g, carbohydrate 37g, fat 36g, saturated fat 12g, fibre 3g, added sugar none, salt 2.72g

Although similar to dumplings in taste,
cobblers are more like scones in texture.

Bacon and Tomato Cobbler

12 rashers streaky or back bacon
1 large onion, chopped
1 tbsp olive oil
4 sticks celery, thickly sliced
350g jar crushed tomatoes
(or 400g can of
chopped tomatoes)
150ml/¼ pint chicken stock
400g can butter beans, drained

FOR THE COBBLER TOPPING
85g/3oz butter
225g/8oz self-raising flour
2 tsp dried mixed herbs
175ml/6fl oz milk

Takes 1¼ hours • Serves 4

1 Preheat the oven to 200°C/Gas 6/fan oven 180°C from cold. Cut three bacon rashers into small pieces and set aside. Cut the rest into three pieces. Fry the onion in the oil for 2–3 minutes, add the large bacon pieces for 5–6 minutes and the celery for 3–4 minutes.
2 Add the tomatoes and stock, bring to the boil, cover and simmer for 20 minutes. Add the beans, then season.
3 To make the cobbler topping, rub the butter into the flour. Stir in the herbs, a pinch of salt and the milk. Put the tomato sauce into a 1.7 litre/3 pint ovenproof dish. Spoon over the topping and scatter over the reserved bacon. Bake for 25–30 minutes until golden.

• Per serving 855 kcalories, protein 31g, carbohydrate 63g, fat 58g, saturated fat 26g, fibre 6g, added sugar none, salt 4.74g

*Ham and vegetables cooked in a mustardy sauce
and topped with shortcrust pastry – great for a crowd.*

Chunky Ham Pie

1 tbsp olive oil
1 onion, chopped
1 garlic clove, crushed
450g/1lb parsnips, roughly chopped
3 carrots, roughly chopped
2 celery sticks, thickly sliced
2 tbsp plain flour
450g/1lb cooked ham,
cut into chunks
142ml carton double cream
425ml/¾ pint vegetable stock
2 tbsp wholegrain mustard
375g packet ready-rolled
shortcrust pastry
a little milk, for brushing
vegetables, to serve

Takes 1¼ hours • Serves 8

1 Preheat the oven to 190°C/Gas 5/fan oven 170°C. Heat the oil in a large pan and cook the onion and garlic for 3–4 minutes. Stir in the parsnips and carrots and cook for 4–5 minutes, stirring frequently. Add the celery, sprinkle in the flour and cook for 1 minute, mixing thoroughly.
2 Add the ham and pour in the cream and stock. Stir in the mustard. Season. Simmer for 5 minutes until slightly thickened, then spoon into a 2 litre/3½ pint dish. Allow to cool slightly.
3 Use the pastry to cover the pie, cutting off any trimmings. Brush with milk. Cut out leaf shapes from the pastry trimmings and put on top of the pie. Brush with milk again and bake for 30 minutes, until the pastry is golden. Serve with vegetables.

• Per serving 452 kcalories, protein 17g, carbohydrate 37g, fat 27g, saturated fat 12g, fibre 5g, added sugar none, salt 2.09g

A risotto cooked as a cake and served in
slices with a good, ready-made tomato sauce.

Pesto Rice Cake

25g/1oz butter
1 large leek (175g/6oz),
finely chopped
350g/12oz risotto rice
1 litre/1¾ pints vegetable stock
100g/4oz green pesto
2 eggs, beaten
150g ball mozzarella, thinly sliced
ready-made tomato sauce, to serve

Takes 1 hour • Serves 4

1 Melt the butter in a frying pan and fry
the leek for 5–6 minutes, until soft. Stir
in the rice. Pour in a ladleful of stock and
simmer until almost all has been absorbed.
Continue to add stock and simmer, stirring
continuously, for 20 minutes or until the rice
is creamy.
2 Stir in the pesto, eggs, and some black
pepper. Spoon half the mixture into a
23cm/9in non-stick frying pan. Arrange the
mozzarella slices on top and spoon over the
remaining rice. Cook over a medium heat for
4 minutes.
3 Put a plate over the frying pan and
carefully invert the rice cake, then slide it
back into the pan. Press to reshape it and
cook for 4 minutes, until golden. Serve with
ready-made tomato sauce.

• Per serving 482 kcalories, protein 19g, carbohydrate
57g, fat 22g, saturated fat 9g, fibre 2g, added sugar
none, salt 1.46g

Just three ingredients,
but still a luxurious finale to a meal.

Lemon Curd Brûlée

568ml carton double cream
225g/8oz good lemon curd
4–5 tsp icing sugar

Takes 15 minutes, plus chilling •
Serves 4

1 In a large bowl, whisk the cream with an electric hand whisk until it just holds its shape, then stir in the lemon curd.
2 Spoon into six 9cm/3½in ramekins and smooth the tops. Chill for at least 1 hour, or overnight if you prefer.
3 Preheat the grill. Sift a thin layer of icing sugar over each ramekin. Grill for about 2–3 minutes until the sugar has caramelised. Alternatively, you can use a blow torch. Serve straight away.

• Per serving 507 kcalories, protein 2g, carbohydrate 12g, fat 50g, saturated fat 32g, fibre none, added sugar 9g, salt 0.09g

It sounds rich but this dessert is surprisingly light.
Make it up to 4 hours ahead of serving.

Coffee Ricotta Creams

4 tbsp raisins
3 tbsp rum or brandy
6 tbsp strong black coffee
50g/2oz caster sugar
250g carton ricotta
142ml carton double cream
50g/2oz dark chocolate, grated
icing sugar, for dusting

Takes 25 minutes, plus chilling •
Serves 4

1 Mix together the raisins, rum or brandy, coffee and sugar. Stir well, then leave for at least 1 hour.

2 Tip the ricotta into a bowl and beat lightly to soften. Gradually beat in the raisins, rum, coffee and sugar mixture. Whip the cream into soft peaks and fold into the ricotta with half the chocolate.

3 Spoon into four glasses and sprinkle over the remaining chocolate. Chill until you are ready to serve. Dust lightly with icing sugar before serving.

• Per serving 447 kcalories, protein 8g, carbohydrate 39g, fat 28g, saturated fat 17g, fibre 1g, added sugar 22g, salt 0.23g

With an original flavour for an ice cream,
this dessert has an unusual but elegant taste.

Iced Ginger Cream

6 ready-made individual meringues
425ml carton double cream
grated zest of 1 lemon
3 tbsp kirsch
2 tbsp caster sugar
4 pieces of stem ginger in syrup,
finely chopped

Takes 20 minutes, plus chilling •
Serves 6

1 Line a 18cm/7in round sandwich cake tin with cling film. Break the meringues into chunks. Whisk the cream until just stiff, then fold in the lemon zest, kirsch, sugar, ginger and meringue pieces.

2 Spoon into the tin, level the top and put in the freezer for at least 4 hours.

3 Turn out of the tin 10 minutes before serving and chill. Cut into wedges and drizzle with the syrup from the jar of ginger.

• Per serving 333 kcalories, protein 2g, carbohydrate 22g, fat 26g, saturated fat 16g, fibre none, added sugar 19g, salt 0.54g

Sharp fruits, cooked in butter and sugar,
make a tempting sauce for ice cream.

Apple Blackberry Ice Cream Sauce

85g/3oz butter
85g/3oz golden caster sugar
4 apples, such as Cox's, peeled,
cored and cut into wedges
100g/4oz blackberries
juice of 1 lemon
vanilla ice cream, to serve

Takes 20 minutes • Serves 4

1 Heat the butter and sugar in a frying pan. When the butter has melted and the sugar has dissolved, stir in the apples.

2 Cook for 5–7 minutes, stirring occasionally, until the apples are tender and the sauce is beginning to caramelise and brown. Immediately remove the pan from the heat and add the blackberries.

3 Stir in the lemon juice and serve spooned over scoops of vanilla ice cream.

• Per serving 302 kcalories, protein 1g, carbohydrate 37g, fat 18g, saturated fat 11g, fibre 3g, added sugar 22g, salt 0.42g

Raid the fruit bowl and the storecupboard
to make a tempting pudding.

Banana Sesame Fritters

100g/4oz self-raising flour
2 tbsp toasted sesame seeds
1 tbsp caster sugar,
plus extra for sprinkling
4 bananas, peeled
vegetable oil, for deep frying
maple syrup, to serve

Takes 30 minutes • Serves 4

1 Mix the flour, sesame seeds and sugar in a bowl. Make a well in the centre and beat in 150ml/¼ pint cold water to make a smooth batter.

2 Cut each banana into four diagonal slices. Fill a large pan or wok a third full with oil and heat until hot. Dip the bananas in the batter, then carefully lower them into the oil with a slotted spoon.

3 Fry for 3–4 minutes until crisp. Drain on kitchen paper. Serve hot, sprinkled with sugar and drizzled with maple syrup.

• Per serving 345 kcalories, protein 5g, carbohydrate 51g, fat 15g, saturated fat 2g, fibre 3g, added sugar 7g, salt 0.26g

Look out for ready-made pancakes in
supermarket chiller or freezer cabinets.

Pancake Streudels

85g/3oz butter
85g/3oz light muscovado sugar
6 eating apples, such as Cox's,
peeled, each cut into 12 wedges
85g/3oz pecans, roughly chopped
85g/3oz raisins
squeeze of lemon juice
6 ready-made pancakes
icing sugar, to dust

Takes 25 minutes • Serves 6

1 Heat the butter and sugar in a frying pan, stirring until dissolved. Toss in the apples and cook, stirring gently, for 3–4 minutes until softened. Add the nuts and let them brown a little.

2 Remove from the heat and stir in the raisins and lemon juice. Spoon some filling into the centre of each pancake.

3 Fold two sides of the pancake into the centre to overlap over the filling slightly. Bring the third side over, then flip the whole pancake over to make a square pouch. Cut in half diagonally and serve with a generous sprinkling of icing sugar.

• Per serving 478 kcalories, protein 6g, carbohydrate 55g, fat 27g, saturated fat 9g, fibre 4g, added sugar 16g, salt 0.41g

Save time with ready-prepared pineapple,
or the canned fruit sold in natural juice.

Baked Pineapple Pudding

1 large pineapple, peeled,
cored and chopped
85g/3oz light muscovado sugar
3 tbsp plain flour
finely grated zest of 1 orange

FOR THE TOPPING
140g/5oz plain flour
50g/2oz ground almonds, toasted
85g/3oz caster sugar
2½ tsp baking powder
¼ tsp salt
1 egg, beaten
5 tbsp natural yogurt
(half a small carton)
85g/3oz butter, melted and cooled
½ tsp vanilla extract
2 tbsp toasted flaked almonds

Takes 1 hour 20 minutes • Serves 6

1 Preheat the oven to 190°C/Gas 5/fan
oven 170°C. Butter a large baking dish.
Put the pineapple, sugar, flour and orange
zest in a bowl and toss well. Spread out in
the dish.
2 Mix together the flour, ground almonds,
sugar, baking powder and salt. Add the egg,
yogurt, butter and vanilla, and stir to combine.
Drop spoonfuls over the fruit, leaving a
2.5cm/1in border.
3 Sprinkle with flaked almondsm. Bake for
50–55 minutes until a skewer inserted in
the centre comes out clean. Serve warm.

• Per serving 492 kcalories, protein 8g, carbohydrate
72g, fat 21g, saturated fat 8g, fibre 4g, added sugar
29g, salt 1.19g

A rich and fruity version of bread and
butter pudding using up buns or fruited loaves.

Hot Cross Bun Pudding

50g/2oz butter
6 hot cross buns, split in half
(fresh or slightly stale)
300ml/½ pint milk
300ml/½ pint single cream
1 tsp vanilla essence
1 tsp ground cinnamon
100g/4oz light muscovado sugar
4 eggs
2 tbsp caster sugar, for sprinkling

Takes 50 minutes • Serves 6

1 Preheat the oven to 180°C/Gas 4/fan
oven 160°C from cold. Butter a 30 × 24cm/
12 × 9½in ovenproof dish, 5cm/2in deep.
Butter the buns and lay them in the dish,
buttered-side up, so they slightly overlap.
Pour the milk and cream into a pan and add
the vanilla essence and half the cinnamon.
Heat gently until it just comes to the boil,
then remove from the heat.
2 In a bowl, whisk together the sugar and
eggs until frothy, then whisk in the warm milk
mixture. Pour evenly over the buns. Leave to
stand for 5 minutes.
3 Sprinkle the remaining cinnamon over
the buns and bake for 30 minutes until set.
Sprinkle over the caster sugar while still warm.

• Per serving 484 kcalories, protein 11g, carbohydrate
57g, fat 25g, saturated fat 14g, fibre 1g, added sugar
30g, salt 0.58g

You can substitute other fruits or fruit mixtures –
fruits of the forest make a nice alternative.

Blueberry and Apple Cobbler

1 Bramley cooking apple,
about 175g/6oz
250g/9oz carton blueberries
50g/2oz light muscovado sugar
250g carton mascarpone

FOR THE COBBLER TOPPING
85g/3oz butter, cut into pieces
225g/8oz self-raising flour
50g/2oz light muscovado sugar
grated zest of 1 lemon
150g carton of natural yogurt

Takes 40 minutes • Serves 6

1 Preheat the oven to 220°C/Gas 7/fan oven 200°C. Peel, core and thinly slice the apple and put into a 1.5 litre/2¾ pint ovenproof dish. Scatter over the blueberries, sprinkle with the sugar and gently stir. Spoon over the mascarpone.

2 To make the topping, rub the butter into the flour or whizz in a food processor until it looks like fine breadcrumbs. Stir in the sugar and lemon zest. Make a well in the centre and tip in the yogurt. Stir until evenly combined, but do not overmix.

3 Spoon the cobbler mixture onto the fruit and mascarpone. Bake for 20 minutes until the topping is risen and golden and the filling is bubbling.

• Per serving 323 kcalories, protein 5g, carbohydrate 49g, fat 13g, saturated fat 8g, fibre 2g, added sugar 17g, salt 0.66g

Don't be put off by the cooking time;
you only need to top up the water once or twice.

Steamed Rhubarb Pudding

350g/12oz rhubarb, cut into chunks
85g/3oz granulated sugar
1 tsp ground ginger
125g/4½oz unsalted butter,
plus extra for greasing
125g/4½oz caster sugar
few drops vanilla extract
2 medium eggs
175g/6oz self-raising flour
cream or custard, to serve

Takes 1 hour 50 minutes • Serves 6

1 Cook the rhubarb, sugar and ginger over a low heat for 3 minutes. Grease a 850ml/ 1½ pint pudding basin and add the rhubarb.
2 Cream the butter and caster sugar together until fluffy. Add the vanilla extract. Beat in the eggs a little at a time, then mix in the flour. Spoon the mixture smoothly onto the rhubarb. Make a pleat across the centre of a piece of buttered greaseproof paper. Place over the basin, butter-side down, cover with foil and tie with string.
3 Place the basin in a large pan and add enough boiling water to half fill the pan. Bring to the boil. Cover and simmer for 1½ hours, topping up the pan with boiling water occasionally. Lift out the basin, remove the coverings and turn the pudding out onto a plate. Serve with cream or custard.

• Per serving 416 kcalories, protein 6g, carbohydrate 58g, fat 20g, saturated fat 11g, fibre 2g, added sugar 35g, salt 0.34g

A spin on old-fashioned treacle tart,
made extra tasty with nuts.

Pecan Tart

25g/1oz self-raising flour
140g/5oz plain flour
85g/3oz cold butter, cut into pieces
pouring cream, to serve

FOR THE FILLING
85g/3oz butter, at room temperature
140g/5oz light muscovado sugar
2 eggs, well beaten
100g/4oz golden syrup
2 tbsp double cream
100g/4oz pecan nuts,
roughly chopped

Takes 1 hour 10 minutes • Serves 8

1 Preheat the oven to 190°C/Gas 5/fan oven 170°C from cold. Rub both the flours and butter into fine crumbs. Add two to three tablespoons of cold water and stir with a palette knife until a dough forms.
2 Shape into a ball, roll out and line a shallow loose-bottomed 23cm/9in fluted flan tin. Bake blind for 17 minutes, then remove the beans and paper. Cook for 5 minutes.
3 To make the filling, beat the butter and sugar until pale and fluffy, then gradually beat in the eggs, syrup and cream. Mix in the nuts. Transfer to the pastry case and bake for 30–35 minutes until set. Cool in the tin and serve with cream.

• Per serving 456 kcalories, protein 5g, carbohydrate 45g, fat 30g, saturated fat 13g, fibre 1g, added sugar 28g, salt 0.58g

Put the biscuits in a plastic bag and
crush them with a rolling pin.

Choc and Ginger Nut Slice

100g/4oz unsalted butter,
plus extra for greasing
185g/7oz plain chocolate
2 tbsp golden syrup
225g/8oz ginger biscuits, crushed
100g/4oz hazelnuts,
toasted and chopped

Takes 20 minutes, plus chilling •
Serves 8

1 Lightly grease a 18cm/7in sandwich tin. In a heatproof bowl set over a pan of simmering water, heat the butter, 100g/4oz chocolate and the syrup, stirring occasionally, until melted.

2 Remove from the heat and stir in the biscuit crumbs and three-quarters of the nuts. Press the mixture into the tin.

3 Melt the remaining chocolate, then spoon on top and sprinkle over the remaining nuts. Chill for 1 hour before serving, cut into slices.

• Per serving 433 kcalories, protein 4g, carbohydrate 39g, fat 30g, saturated fat 13g, fibre 2g, added sugar 20g, salt 0.68g

Use porridge oats for a chewy result,
or jumbo oats for a crunchy finish.

Classic Oat Flapjacks

175g/6oz butter, cut into pieces
140g/5oz golden syrup
50g/2oz light muscovado sugar
250g/9oz oats

Takes 35 minutes • Serves 12

1 Preheat the oven to 180°C/Gas 4/fan oven 160°C from cold. Line the base of a shallow 23cm/9in square tin with a sheet of baking parchment.
2 Put the butter, syrup and sugar in a medium pan. Stir over a low heat until the butter has melted and the sugar has dissolved. Remove from the heat and stir in the oats.
3 Press the mixture into the tin. Bake for 20–25 minutes, until golden brown on top. Allow to cool in the tin for 5 minutes, then mark into bars or squares with the back of a knife while still warm. Cool in the tin completely before cutting and removing – this prevents the flapjack from breaking up.

• Per serving 242 kcalories, protein 3g, carbohydrate 29g, fat 14g, saturated fat 8g, fibre 1g, added sugar 13g, salt 0.38g

Index

Picture credits and recipe credits

BBC Worldwide would like to thank the following for providing photographs. While every effort has been made to trace and acknowledge all photographers, we would like to apologise should there be any errors or omissions.

Chris Alack p71, p79, p91, p93; Marie-Louise Avery p53, p117; Jean Cazals p155, p187, p189; Ken Field p87, p115, p125; Dave King p75, p173, p183; William Lingwood p197; David Munns p41, p45, p49, p69, p105, p129, p135, p145, p147, p191, p199, p209; William Reavell p19, p157; Howard Shooter p57; Simon Smith p37, p111; Roger Stowell p15, p17, p21, p25, p27, p31, p33, p35, p39, p43, p51, p59, p61, p63, p65, p67, p77, p81, p85, p87, p95, p97, p101, p103, p113, p119, p123, p127, p131, p133, p137, p139, p149, p151, p159, p163, p165, p167, p169, p175, p177, p179, p181, p193, p195, p201; Sam Stowell p141, p143; Martin Thompson p11, p13, p23, p29, p47, p55, p83, p121, p161, p171; Martin Thompson and Philip Webb p73, p99; Ian Wallace p207; Philip Webb p211; Simon Wheeler p89, p107; Jonathan Whitaker p203; BBC Worldwide p153, p185, p205

All the recipes in this book have been created by the editorial teams on *BBC Good Food Magazine* and *BBC Vegetarian Good Food Magazine*.

Angela Boggiano, Lorna Brash, Sara Buenfeld, Mary Cadogan, Gilly Cubitt, Barney Desmazery, Joanna Farrow, Rebecca Ford, Silvana Franco, Catherine Hill, Jane Lawrie, Clare Lewis, Sara Lewis, Liz Martin, Kate Moseley, Orlando Murrin, Vicky Musselman, Angela Nilsen, Justine Pattison, Jenny White and Jeni Wright.